STRANGER IN MY HOME

C. Raymond Holmes

POINTER PUBLICATIONS

10623 RED BUD TRAIL
BERRIEN SPRINGS, MICH. 49103

DEDICATED

to the memory of
seven fruitful and happy years
as pastor of
Sharon Lutheran Church
Bessemer, Michigan

TABLE OF CONTENTS

PREFACE

Since the first edition of *Stranger In My Home* went out of print numerous inquiries have been received concerning the future availability of the book. For that reason, and because the book has been instrumental in the decisions of many people to join the Seventh-day Adventist Church, its republication was undertaken.

Two goals were established for this second edition: (1) A complete revision of the existing text which would include improving language and expression, updating and correcting certain data, and adding significant and pertinent new details that would expand the readers perception of events as they took place; and (2) An enlargement by adding two chapters covering events subsequent to my baptism into the Seventh-day Adventist Church, and an assessment of Adventism after sixteen years.

The rewriting, together with the new material, has served to reaffirm my confidence in God's guidance, and also increase my faith in the Biblical doctrines held by the SDA Church which I have continued to explore in connection with preaching and teaching.

Once again I am indebted to many people: Lutherans who continue to be my friends, parishioners of the Adventist tradition, students of the Seventh-day Adventist Theological Seminary in the Philippines and at Berrien Springs, Michigan, and colleagues in pastoral and teaching ministry. All have served to sharpen my faith and perception concerning what God has done in the fulfillment of His promise to me in Jeremiah 29:11.

My special thanks to Mrs. Hedwig Jemison, a queen among Adventist women, for her perceptive editorial assistance, and to William Fagal for assisting with the computer formatting of the text for printing.

This second edition is offered with the prayer that the Holy Spirit will continue to use it to touch the hearts of people who are looking for a spiritual home in which the Word of God is central for faith and life.

Andrews University
Berrien Springs, Michigan

INTRODUCTION

Summer in Michigan's Upper Peninsula was beautiful that year, so warm and pleasant. The rainfall was just right, causing the many gardens and flower beds in our small town of Bessemer, which had lain fallow for the long winter, to flourish. On a soft evening in July of that unforgettable summer, a group of twelve people, meeting regularly for prayer and fellowship, gathered in the backyard of one member of Sharon Lutheran Church. A gentle breeze blew from the north bringing with it a cool touch from Canada as it swept over Lake Superior, seasoned with the delicate fragrance of the pine forest that covers so much of that beautiful piece of God's creation.

As I watched them arrive, I was aware of their earnestness and commitment to Jesus Christ. Over the years, as they responded to the Word of God, they had become very precious to me. I called them "my grapes," the fruit of my ministry. For seven years I had the unspeakable privilege of being their pastor, their spiritual shepherd. Those were fruitful years in the history of that congregation, and for me too. The years in Bessemer taught me many valuable spiritual lessons as I matured in my own faith and in ministry.

But soon I would have to leave them and the thought was hard to bear. God was once again revealing a new direction in the "race" He had set before me some sixteen years earlier. That evening I would have to tell them how God was leading and directing my life in what surely would appear to be as strange and disturbing to them as it was to me.

It was essential to honor their trust in me as their spiritual leader by being as open and candid as possible. I had to share fully what was happening to me and my family, because there are times when we must take the risks that are part of exposing the reality of God's activity in our lives. Only in this way does His church grow strong in faith and service. Faith and trust must undergo testing from time to time and without a doubt God was testing me. But at the same time He wanted to test them too. Unbeknown to them God was bringing us to a moment of truth and decision. Events over the next year and a half in Bessemer would reveal to them the alternatives they faced.

There was no way to know if that group of people would understand what I felt I must do, or even make an attempt to comprehend. But I trusted their love for, and confidence in, me. While each of them would ultimately respond to my story in different ways, none of them disappointed me in the long run.

Several understood readily that I must follow what I believed to be God's direction. Some could not understand, and never would, but promised to try. Others felt I was making the greatest mistake of my life, but trusted me to God and promised to pray for me. A few would eventually follow the way I would go. What more could I ask of them? They offered all they had at the moment. Their Christian love and ministry to me at a most difficult time will never be forgotten. It helped me immensely during the critical months ahead.

In the hush of that evening around a glowing fire as I told them at least part of the story of this book, I rejoiced in the realization that even in that situation the Holy Spirit would lead my precious friends ever deeper in their relationship with Christ. I knew that as surely as He was guiding me, He would take them another step in their individual walks with Him. I began to speak.

Early in my perplexity and struggle a passage from the prophet Jeremiah held special significance for me: "I know the plans I have for you, says the Lord, plans for welfare and not for evil, to give you a future and a hope." (Jeremiah 29:11) God has a will and a plan for every single human life. It is a good plan. Its goals are lofty and high because they are His goals, and are impossible to attain apart from His divine help. He reveals His will and plan, not in its totality, but step by step. The road ahead may at times seem curved and obscure, but God brightly illuminates each single step. When one takes each step in faith, He illuminates the next and gently bids us go forward.

God often leads more directly by arranging circumstances in such a way that one cannot avoid making certain decisions. Still we must seek His will by searching His Word and by prayer. We must ascertain all the facts and think carefully through the circumstances as free from prejudice and self-will as possible. Finally, one must take "a leap of faith." Such moments of decision are never easy. They aren't intended to be. God wants us to exercise the faith He has given in order to strengthen that faith for the future and to learn to depend on His trustworthiness.

I wrote the book you are about to read for those who have difficulty believing that God so personally involves Himself in each life that He actually guides it. Some believe that God does have a will or divine plan, but that a person cannot determine what it is. This book is my witness to the fact that He not only has a will for each life, but that it can be known. It is also my confession of faith in His daily guidance since He first found me in 1953-54.

My hope and prayer is that in sharing my story you will find encouragement as you seek to surrender your life to His will for you.

I, alone, am responsible for the contents of this volume, but I could never have written it without the encouragement of Mrs. Hedwig Jemison, Dr. Thomas Blincoe, of Andrews University, and Dr. Wilber Alexander, now of Loma Linda University. My gratitude extends also to Mrs. Roland Anderson, who labored at the task of typing the manuscript. I would like to extend a special word of appreciation to Elder James Hayward, senior pastor of the Battle Creek Tabernacle, who so graciously allowed me the necessary time to complete the book while serving as his associate. In the background stand numerous individuals, friends, and members of my former parishes who have supported my family and me in love and in prayer. What they have meant to me defies adequate description. All have contributed in some way to the story you are about to read.

1

A FATEFUL SATURDAY

It was Saturday morning. As I did every Saturday, I walked up the street from the old parsonage where we lived to the familiar brick church and entered Kastman Hall, where my office was located, named after one of my predecessors whose ministry in that congregation extended over 24 years. Paneled in rich birch, carpeted with a bright green rug, furnished with a large walnut desk and comfortable executive chair, the room's pleasant atmosphere was conducive to study, meditation, and prayer. Sunday's sermon, entitled "The Need For Prayer," rested unfinished on the desk. After more meditation on the Biblical text, I turned to the typewriter and began to complete the notes for the sermon I would preach to my waiting congregation the next morning:

> There are moments in the believer's life when all he can do is pray. Words which he has become so used to using fail him completely. He knows not where to turn. Fear has covered him like a thick, smothering blanket. His heart is near to breaking and feels heavy in his breast. All of his human resources fail completely. Intelligence, education, common sense, and talents are rendered useless in the face of odds so great that retreat and defeat become appealing, for they will at least bring rest. To his knees he goes with but one plea, 'God be merciful to me!' He pleads for strength, for courage, for faith to believe that God does not go back on His promises, for faith to believe that He does not bring a person so far and then chop him off as if nothing had happened in the past.

1

AGONIZING EVENTS

With a feeling of satisfaction I closed my Bible, replaced the cover on the typewriter, and left for home. Little did I know how much I, the preacher would need those words the next morning! Little did I know how prophetic they would be! Nor could I know what an agonizing, soul-wrenching series of events would begin within the next five minutes--events that would bring my faith its most severe test, that would stretch near to breaking the cords that bound my family together, that would test my ministry and the faith of my congregation.

I was happy and content in my calling as pastor and teacher of the Word of God. Though I struggled with the problems connected with a meager salary my life overflowed with meaning and purpose. Moments later when I entered my home, I expected to find my wife, Shirley, busy preparing the noon meal. Instead, I found a babysitter with David and Rhoda, our two children. Surprised, and somewhat puzzled, I asked where their mother had gone. They did not know, except that she had left a few moments before with Mrs. Bertha, *Bert*, Bigford.

Saturday morning!

It could mean only one thing! My heart pounded with apprehension as I ran to my car and sped off to the next town, five miles away, where Dr. and Mrs. Bigford attended church. They were Seventh-day Adventists. The car raced to catch up with my thoughts. Why is she doing this? Had she become discontented with the religious life of our church? With my preaching?

No! Impossible! It must be just a visit to a friend's church. But I could not talk myself out of the terrible sense of foreboding that possessed me. In my entire life I had never known such fear. The thought of what Shirley's trip to the Bigford's church might mean terrified me. The implications, the consequences of what I feared, were unthinkable and assaulted my senses. I groaned audibly. My hands trembled as I drove. So much was at stake! I just had to catch up with them. She couldn't do such a thing to me! She wouldn't! How could she? Anger began to mix with fear.

I saw them cross the intersection just ahead and frantically waved them to the curb. They watched intently, not moving, as I approached the car and wrenched open the door.

"Where are you going?" I demanded to know.
"To church," Shirley softly answered.
"Why?"
"I just want to go to church with my friend."
"But why?"
No answer. They looked at each other.

My heart sank, for then I knew. My worst fears had become reality. With trembling voice I asked, *"Do I have something to worry about?"*

Shirley looked up at me and replied, *"Yes, I guess you do."*

Stifling an uncontrollable sob, I demanded that she get out of the car and come home with me at once. *Bert* insisted that I could not stop Shirley from worshipping as she chose. Curtly I told her to stop meddling in our affairs. Deep and passionate resentment of her influence welled up within me like a poisoned spring. I could almost taste it. At that moment I hated her with a fierceness I did not know I possessed, for instinctively I sensed the enormous difficulties the situation would cause.

Fortunately, and wisely, Shirley agreed to come home. We dismissed the sitter and began the first in a long and painful series of disagreeable scenes lasting almost two years.

I demanded to know what she thought she was doing! What had happened during the previous week which the two friends spent together at an Adventist camp meeting? Had she been gullible and stupid enough to fall for such an unsophisticated and ridiculous theology? Didn't she realize, with her pietistic Lutheran training and insight, that the Adventist "sect" represented legalism? Having grown so beautifully in her Christian faith and experience, was she now about to slip back under the demands of the law? Having begun "in the Spirit" like the Galatians, was she now "ending in the flesh?" How could she think of accepting the Jewish Sabbath when Christ had set her free from the works of the law?

While I ranted and vented my anger, she sat silent. What had happened to her? Had she been brainwashed by some clever and manipulative evangelist? Had she lost her mind? Didn't she realize the position her behaviour would place me in? What it would do to our family? How divisive

3

it would be? What about my future in the ministry? Had she considered the possible consequences to my ministerial career at all? I gave no chance for her to explain, made no attempt to understand. All I could see was the impossible situation her actions had brought upon me.

SATANIC ATTACK

How was I to interpret what was happening? I considered the whole episode an attack by Satan on my ministry. What more vulnerable spot could there be than a minister's own home and family? If Satan could disrupt my home, occupy my mind and energy, he would have me in his power and could destroy every bit of good accomplished during the previous five years. He had seduced my wife with a false theology that he was using to "capture weak women . . . who will listen to anybody." (2 Tim. 3:6-7)

All who belonged to the Bigford's religion, I was rapidly convinced, were Satan's unholy angels seeking to break up homes and wreck the ministries of Bible-believing men. I believed that one of the marks of earth's last days, just before Christ's second coming, would be the rise of many false prophets and counterfeit religious systems. As far as I was concerned, the Bigford's church was one of those groups.

Arguments, lectures, pleas, failed to alter Shirley's mind. It was one of those occasions when her stubborn Finnish courage, called *sisu,* manifested itself. She proceeded to observe the seventh-day Sabbath. Almost immediately her life-style began to change and she became a stranger in my home.

2

THE BEGINNING

Finland, a small country located north of Estonia, east across the Baltic Sea from Sweden, and west of the Soviet Union, is a land of stately pines, white birch, many lakes, and short summers contrasting with long and severe winters. It is a land of hardy people. Despite the severity of the climate, they are lovers of nature, an outdoor people. Those who are religious exhibit a deep piety and an unshakable faith, immovable in conviction. Fiercely independent, they resist domination. But friendship, love, and loyalty given freely, are permanent.

Such is the land and the people from which we come, Shirley and I. Her ancestors were pure Finns, coming from the central part of Finland. Mine were Swedish-speaking Finns from the western coast, not far from the old city of Vaasa. Farmers, our forebears worked the soil hard during the short growing season, and experienced quite a few lean years. Some of those lean years, shortly before the turn of the century, caused Shirley's parents, my grandparents, and my father to immigrate to America.

I was born on May 14, 1929, in Waukegan, Illinois, also the hometown of the famous comedian Jack Benny. In fact my childhood home was just a few short blocks from the apartment building where he lived as a boy. My father earned his living as a bricklayer and was building a home when I was born, just steps away from the empty lot where later he and I would build the church in which I would find the Lord and be married one day. The great depression lurked just around the corner of time, and when it came my father lost his job and his home.

5

FATHER'S COUNSEL

In 1947 I graduated from Waukegan Township High and since I had no idea what to do, my father insisted I learn the mason trade. The next day I was on the job for 50 cents an hour. His insistence was providential. His discipline and the experience of working with skilled craftsmen gradually helped me develop confidence. When it came to the trade he was a good teacher by word and example.

He taught me his ethics and common sense approach to life. "Always be honest," he would say. "You'll never get so old that you can't learn something new everyday." "Don't ever let me hear that you got fired for doing a poor job." Himself a master bricklayer, he insisted that I become one too. My work had to be the equal of his, if not better. Once I built a chimney slightly out of plumb and he kicked it down, pointed at me and said "Do it again and do it right!"

Eventually I started a small mason contracting business of my own that by 1953-54 was well on the way to success. My advertisements read "FOR A BETTER HOME SEE HOLMES," and I had big plans for the future. But Someone else had bigger plans.

CONVERSION

When I think back on my childhood and youth, I can't remember giving God one serious thought, not even during my mother's illness and death in 1948. There was no God as far as I was concerned. But gradually I began to sense an emptiness within me. Although construction offered lucrative and creative work, inwardly I was restless and dissatisfied. Life didn't have much meaning. I know now that God was beginning to work in my heart. "There must be more to life than what I know," I told myself. "Somewhere lies meaning and purpose to existence."

I began to struggle with questions ignored for years when some friends invited me to attend mid-week youth programs at a Baptist church. After a few meetings I began to go to the Sunday morning services, but didn't appreciate the pressure put on me by some of the earnest-minded people concerned about my spiritual condition, or what I instinctively felt was superficial preaching. However, having my attention drawn to the Christian faith, I decided to look into

6

it further. Perhaps, I concluded, I ought to start where I was baptized as an infant, the Lutheran Church.

There, in the church my father and I had built, I began to open my ears and heart to the message of Christianity. During the next year, under excellent Lutheran evangelical and expository preaching, I came to know Jesus Christ as my Saviour and Lord. It thrilled me each day to open the Bible and find relevant instruction, counsel, and spiritual food for my soul. Excitedly I sensed the indwelling presence of Christ and experienced victory over sin, over despondency, and over the meaninglessness of my life.

SHIRLEY

Laying brick became a holy task. My new patience amazed me. I took catechetical instruction, and was received into membership at St. Mark's Lutheran Church. Soon I found myself in the choir with a young woman to whom my cousin, who happened to be married to her brother, introduced me. She was a Finn from Upper Michigan. A lover of sports she wore a white sailor hat with the brim turned down, peddle-pushers, and energetically rode a bicycle everywhere.

A Christian all her life, she can never remember a time when she did not believe in Jesus Christ as her Saviour. Born in Wakefield, Michigan, she grew up in the environment of a Christian home. Although it was difficult to raise a large family in the 1920's and 30's, her family included twelve children. Both of her parents were previously married. Her father's first wife died in a flu epidemic, and her mother's first husband perished in a mine disaster. The family thus consisted of three groups of children, humorously referred to as "my kids, your kids, and our kids." Each group consisted of four children, Shirley being the youngest of them all.

Shirley and her mother were kindred spirits and shared deep thoughts with each other. Anna Jarvinen was the spiritual soul and fiber of the family, while David provided the necessary rock-like stability. Both of Shirley's parents were baptized as infants in the Finnish Lutheran State Church and underwent the rigorous catechetical exercises common in those days. They memorized Luther's *Small Catechism* and many passages from Scripture. Late in life they could still quote from the catechism and creeds. The

7

deep pietism of the Finnish revival movements nurtured their faith. They loved the Word of God, and in later years David Jarvinen would read aloud from the large family Bible. From his retirement until his death he read the Bible through in this way at least three times.

The Jarvinens had a deep and abiding love for the Lutheran Church. It was instilled in childhood as they responded to the call of the church bell and even through winter snowdrifts found their way to the house of God. There they learned the stately hymns of the church and the beloved songs of the Finnish Lutheran awakenings, some with as many as fifteen verses.

One of Shirley's fondest memories is of attending worship services with her parents. She recalls with nostalgia the sight of her father's large, work-scarred hands folded in prayer. As a small child she received instruction about the sanctity of the church building and the behavior that sanctity required. She must not speak, but sit quietly and attentively with her eyes always on the pastor, listening closely to the sermon which sometimes lasted an hour or more. At the age of thirteen she became a member of the congregation by means of the rite of confirmation.

After graduation from high school, Shirley left home for a one-year business course and then to Waukegan to work at Great Lakes Naval Training Center.

Our meeting was certainly providential in that it took place about the same time I began to attend St. Mark's Lutheran Church. While my conversion to Christ came about through the preaching of the Word of God, her warm and convicting personal testimony was influential too. Most of our dates involved church affairs or dinner at a restaurant, and we would talk for hours. During those hours of conversation I gradually became aware of, and began to articulate for the first time, the things I believed. It is amazing how one can remain unconscious of the depth of convictions until given the opportunity to share them. Those conversations helped me to formulate and systematize my new faith. After more than thirty years of marriage we have not run out of conversation, most of it of a spiritual nature.

THE CALL

In June 1953, the Finnish Evangelical Lutheran Church held its annual convention in Waukegan. Once again divine providence arranged significant circumstances. The choir of St. Mark's, in which both Shirley and I sang, was invited to participate in the festive service of ordination, the climax of the convention.

As I listened to the powerful sermon and witnessed the laying on of hands as six young men knelt for ordination, God spoke inwardly to me about ministry. Later that night, unable to fall asleep, I laughed it off as a silly whim. However, as the days and weeks went by, the thought intensified until it literally filled my mind every hour of each day. I didn't dare tell a soul. It was too unbelievable, too impossible! But it intensified until I would lie awake at night thinking what it would mean, what major decisions I would have to make, what dramatic changes would take place in my life. It was overwhelming.

Finally I went to see my pastor. He listened closely as I related what was happening and began to smile. It turned out that he had given my name to the admissions office of Suomi College[1] in Hancock, Michigan, as a possible ministerial student. He asked them to send me a catalog and thought it might arrive that very day. Needless to say, I raced home and hopefully opened the mailbox. There it was! My heart leaped as I realized how God was arranging circumstances and clearly pointing the way.

It didn't take long to fill out the application, mail it, and begin to phase out my construction business and plan my departure.

OFF TO COLLEGE

At the age of twenty-four I left for college in September, 1954. Fearfully and apprehensively I approached a new phase of life. From Waukegan, Illinois to Hancock, Michigan is a long day's drive, and the closer I got to Suomi College the more apprehensive I became. Never a scholar in high school, graduating by the literal skin of my teeth, the first

---

[1] Suomi College, the name means "Finland," was a two-year liberal arts college started by immigrant Finns in the 19th century primarily to train ministers for the young church in America. By the time I attended it had an excellent academic reputation and its graduates were accepted into major universities.

six weeks were miserable. The first exams were flops, I flunked them all! Totally discouraged, I felt certain that I was making a grave mistake, and began to consider dropping out of school. Then one fall day the Lord revealed His will in a delightful way. While seated in the library, attempting to read a textbook on American history but actually making plans to leave for home that very day, a hand reached over my shoulder and propped a white card against my book. "I can do all things through Christ which strengtheneth me," the card read. (Philippians 4:13) As I turned to see who had been so perceptive, my history professor was going through the door. Bless that man! His concern and sensitivity to a floundering student's needs touched me deeply. "Surely," I thought, "with such love and friendship all things are possible." That's what it is like to study at a Christian school, where the concern is not just to fill the brain with ideas but to fill the heart with faith and trust in the goodness of God.

A few weeks later, when I needed another touch from God, He sent a message through another person. It was a cold and rainy day in early winter. The clouds were as dark and heavy as they can be so far north. My heart felt the same way as I stood looking out the chapel window. I thought I was alone until I heard a familiar pastoral voice behind me say: "Isn't it wonderful to know that above all those clouds the sun is shining?" It was the pastor of the local Lutheran Church who had come to speak in chapel that morning. Suddenly I became starkly aware of the weakness of my faith, and realized that God was actually testing that faith in preparation for what might lay ahead. With renewed confidence and determination I turned with vigor to my studies, because I knew that God was with me and would see me through. He was meeting my needs.

MARRIAGE

Overjoyed at the dramatic improvement in my grades, I got the courage to ask Shirley to become my wife. We met in Wakefield for Thanksgiving and went for a walk in a snowstorm. Stopping under an Indianhead sign on the road around Sunday Lake I "popped" the question. Engaged at Christmas, we married the following June, 1955. That fall we moved into a tiny apartment near the college.

We had no idea how we would furnish an apartment for the second year in college until the day I found seven hundred dollars! Actually I didn't really "find" it. It was the result of a bookkeeping mistake as I phased out my business the previous fall. In closing my checking account I left a balance of forty dollars to pay a public accountant for estimating my income tax in the spring. When I called on him at Easter, he had everything prepared. I asked him if the account had sufficient funds to cover his fee. He said there was more than enough. I asked what the balance was and he answered, "Seven hundred dollars." A simple error of neglecting to enter some deposits, with such happy consequences! Was it the providence of God? I took it as further evidence that I was on the right road in His plan for my life.

After completing the second year at Suomi College, we moved to Marquette, Michigan, where I enrolled at Northern Michigan University. Since we could find no available apartments, we sold our furniture and began to pray that the Lord would help us find housing for the fall. We spent the summer in Waukegan, where I worked laying brick. Meanwhile, we decided that the only feasible housing would be a travel trailer. Apartment rents were impossibly high in Marquette in relation to our estimated income. But we had no funds for a trailer. However, a sad event, the death of my grandfather, made available a bequest amounting to $2,000.

For weeks we hunted for a suitable trailer the right size, in reasonably good condition, and at a price within our budget. We found nothing. What we saw was too old, too big, too dilapidated, or too expensive. Then one evening we decided to stop at another trailer agency. After looking at everything in sight we started to drive away in disappointment, when Shirley happened to glimpse a small blue trailer hidden behind the rest. Upon our inquiry the salesman said he thought we wouldn't be interested in that one. But we were! It was the right size, clean, and in perfect condition. We knew it was "our" trailer, but hardly dared to ask the price. Imagine our happiness when told it was $1,800! We made the deal on the spot, once again knowing that God's providential hand was on our lives taking care of every need.

With confident faith we pulled our new "home" to Marquette to begin the second phase of my education and preparation for ministry. Shirley needed a job and in this the Lord also provided. Passing me in the hall one day the dean of students stopped and inquired if my wife needed a job. Upon my affirmative answer, he made a personal recommendation for her at the office of the superintendent of public schools. There she worked for the next two years completing her undergraduate PHT--Putting Hubby Through.

SEMINARY

Graduation from Northern Michigan University took place in late May, 1958, and my diploma read, "With Distinction," the equivalent of *magna cum laude*. Philippians 4:13 was true! By faith and trust in God the impossible is possible. He brings His promises to pass. Nothing is too hard for Him. Over and over again He proved His absolute trustworthiness to me. In such a way He taught me how to have complete confidence in Him and in His written Word. How important and crucial such reliance would be in the future, I had no way of knowing at the time.

The Finnish Evangelical Lutheran Church had been engaged for some time in merger discussions with three other church bodies: The United Lutheran Church, the Augustana Lutheran Church, and the American Evangelical Lutheran Church. As a by-product of those discussions, in the summer of 1957, the Finnish Church voted to transfer its seminary from Hancock, Michigan, and affiliate it with Chicago Lutheran Theological Seminary located in Maywood, Illinois, a suburb of Chicago. For a long time I had misgivings about the proposed merger of churches and about the move of the seminary to Maywood. The Maywood seminary had the reputation of being theologically liberal. Certain that my church was making a grave mistake in judgment, I made plans to enroll in a more conservative and orthodox Lutheran seminary in Minneapolis.

Securing the application forms I filled them out, addressed and stamped the envelope, and placed it in my briefcase for mailing. Each day for two weeks as I attempted to mail it, something made me hesitate. Each time I opened the mailbox, I could not insert the envelope. Finally, almost in desperation, and certainly with apprehension, I filled out an application to the Maywood, Illinois, seminary and was able, without hindrance of any kind, to mail it immediately.

We arrived in Maywood in September 1958. I remember wondering how it was possible that I should be there instead of Minneapolis. However, determined that God would have His way, I trusted in Him once again. Immediately He began to assure me that I was indeed in His divine plan. The day after our arrival Shirley received an unsolicited job offer as assistant librarian in the seminary library. It meant that she would not have to commute into Chicago each day and that we could take our meals together in the cafeteria. Once again she did not have to seek employment.

Finding our place in the atmosphere of the seminary was difficult. Our pietistic approach to the Christian life was looked upon by many not only as strange but offensive. By "pietistic" I mean the Lutheran heritage passed down from the Pietistic movements and revivals in Europe and Finland. They had come about as a reaction against rationalism and its emphasis on intellectual acceptance of doctrine and little emphasis on personal Christian experience during certain periods of Lutheran history. I remember the day when I left our room for class and saw flying from the campus flagpole a crude banner made from a white sheet. On it was painted in red letters "Down With Piety!"

The prevailing attitude toward Christian life-style at the seminary troubled us. It was hard for us to understand how faith in Christ could be confessed with so little consideration for sanctification. It shocked us to see ministerial students using alcoholic beverages. The difference in life-style between us grew out of basic theological differences. Suffice it to say, the three seminary years were difficult yet rewarding. We made many friends. Most important of all, God used the environment, the discussions, even the differences, to fortify and confirm my convictions about the Gospel, the nature of the Christian life, the ministry, and about the inspiration and reliability of His Word.

ORDINATION

Graduation took place in early May, 1961, and we moved a few days later to our first parish. I was called to serve three congregations at Trout Creek, Paynesville, and Ewen, in Michigan's Upper Peninsula. On June 25, 1961, the Finnish Evangelical Lutheran Church ordained me during the annual convention, held that year in Fairport Harbor, Ohio.

We moved into an almost empty and very old parsonage, except for the kitchen furnishings, the bedroom set, a rocking chair, and two folding camp cots in the living room.

My office furniture consisted of a desk that I made from a door, and an old chair resurrected from the ancient and unused garage in the backyard. But that was unimportant when compared with the excitement of beginning the work for which I had spent seven long years in preparation.

3

THE CALL TO MINISTER

During the years in seminary I developed my theology more fully and came to some definite conclusions with respect to ministry and discipleship. The reader needs to understand them to see how they affected my reaction to Shirley's eventual interest in the Seventh-day Adventist Church.

BIBLE AS AUTHORITY

I gradually realized that the Bible must be more than a devotional book for a preacher. Soon I would have to preach and teach the Bible. To do so, I had to answer a basic question forced upon me by the kind of theology I was hearing every day. The answer would have serious implications for my faith and ministry. "Is the Bible in any sense revelation from God?"--I asked. If it was not, then it was not worth the bother and I could devote my life to a study of history or literature. However, if it was in fact revelation from God, then my course would be clear.

I began to read it with that question in mind. As I traced the accounts of history recorded in the Old Testament and saw how God acted time and time again on behalf of His people, and how that history pointed toward the Messianic Age, I began to discern His voice. The conviction grew that the Bible was not merely a compilation of the writings of men who had reached a certain degree of holiness, but, rather, God revealing Himself in acts of history recorded by inspired men themselves involved in that history. Nor was it simply a collection of interpretations of those historic events that applied only to the times in which they were written. The New Testament, for example, was not just the early church's witness and understanding of the revelation of Christ. It was revelation.

A minister must be able to preach and teach with authority. That authority must come from a reliable source, or no one will heed it. It cannot rest on personal experience, but must have firm roots in an objective and reliable norm applicable for all time. That norm is the written Word of God, the Bible.

The next question was, Where did the message of the Bible come from? 2 Timothy 3:16 says that "all scripture is inspired by God and profitable for teaching." 2 Peter 1:21 states that "no prophecy ever came by the impulse of man, but men moved by the Holy Spirit spoke from God." The apostle Paul states clearly that he did not receive his message from the culture of his day, nor from the Rabbinic tradition, nor was it his personal opinion. He said:

> For I would have you know, brethren, that the gospel which was preached by me is not man's gospel. For I did not receive it from man, nor was I taught it, but it came through a revelation of Jesus Christ. (Gal. 1:11-12)

My conviction grew that the Bible is indeed the Word of God, inspired by Him, and therefore infallible concerning its message. The Bible writers spoke with the authority of the Lord and expected believers to obey it. (2 Thess. 3:14) The Holy Spirit did not dictate the Bible word by word to its writers, He gave them principles of truth and they expressed it in their own way. But their expression cannot be separated from the source. The human writers of the Bible wrote what they meant and meant what they wrote.

When we read the Bible, we can know that what it contains is there because it is the truth. The Written Word brings us into contact with the Truth that lies behind it, Jesus Christ. We, with our imperfect and finite minds, cannot arrogantly dissect the Bible in order to arrive at truth. Rather, we must place ourselves beneath that Word and allow it to address us where we are. Only by understanding the Bible in such a way can the minister preach it. Only then will those who come to hear him experience transformed lives and characters.

Many things in the Bible may escape our comprehension, but that doesn't mean they are not truth. Truth is not dependant upon our understanding of it. The Bible promises, however, that the Holy Spirit will not only reveal the truth, but will lead us into all truth (John 14:18-26). As one walks with God by faith in His Son, knowledge of God's revelation increases. As a result he must bring his life more and more into harmony with the revealed will of God.

CONFRONTATION WITH LIBERALISM

During my seminary training I came face to face with a liberal approach to the doctrine of reconciliation. That approach, containing elements of humanism and universalism, taught that people do not need to be reconciled to God through conversion, because the objective, historical act of Christ on the cross has already reconciled them. They simply need to be told that they are indeed reconciled.

I recall hearing one of my professors, who taught Pastoral Psychology, say that all the pastor can do in the face of the sin problems of his people is show them that he loves them and accepts them as they are. Repeatedly I raised the question, "But what about the ministry of reconciliation?" He gave no answer. "What about the transforming power of the Gospel? What about the new birth?" Still no answer. In his view there was no need for personal reconciliation with God through repentance and surrender to Christ when there is the objective fact of the cross and the sacraments to bring its benefits. But I knew that such a concept does not lead to transformation of life and character.

Christ did not die on the cross so that we can learn to live with our sin. He died in order that we might have victory over sin. When the Lord forgave the woman caught in adultery and set her on her feet, He went much further than accepting her as she was. He forgave her sin and then sent her on her way with the admonition not to sin again. It is only the redeemed and forgiven sinner who can experience victory over sin, because Christ does not command the impossible. What He commands, He gives grace, the divine strength and ability, to do. That's justification by faith and sanctification by faith. And "by faith" does not mean just an intellectual or mental assent, but a complete surrender of the life to God. Both justification and sanctification are necessary in the Christian's experience, both are part of reconciliation. Without reconciliation man has no

17

salvation, and without sanctification he has no victory over sins.

THE DOCTRINE OF SANCTIFICATION

As my realization of this truth developed, I began to get more concerned about the doctrine of sanctification and the experience of sanctification in the believer's life. The Christian life consists of more than being justified by grace. To be sure, God cannot save anyone from the power and curse of sin unless that individual surrenders in faith to His act of justification in Jesus Christ. But God also saves him *for* something, "to be conformed to the image of his Son." (Romans 8:29)

I had a difficult time with the doctrine of sanctification during my seminary years. The theological emphasis in the school centered around a one-sided consideration of justification with little concern for sanctification. The life-style of many of the students showed the results of such an emphasis. The few who believed the Christian must take what God wants to do *in us* as seriously as what He has done *for us* received criticism as synergists or pietists. Synergism is the idea that God and I, in cooperation, achieve sanctification. Pietism, understood wrongly, makes the Christian life appear as a sad list of do's and don'ts. Many seminarians saw both as legalistic self-efforts at holiness.

It is easy to forget that what God wants accomplished *in us*, He, by His Spirit, undertakes to do *for us*. Why one could not accept this by faith, equally as well as justification, I could not understand. But I came to the conclusion that a lack of growth in sanctification in the Christian's experience leaves him in danger of losing salvation itself. One cannot stand still in the Christian experience. What doesn't grow, dies. The physical body which never reaches maturity, never knows full and complete life. The mind which does not develop cannot function properly. By the same token, faith which does not grow cannot bring forth the fruits of righteousness as God intended. Christianity is far more than a body of truth; it is a way of life.

To surrender to Jesus Christ by faith means to give up all attempts to attain righteousness and to permit Him to give it to us. It means laying down our own struggles for goodness and simply accepting what Jesus Christ gives. We turn our entire lives over to Him to do with as He pleases.

18

Jesus Christ becomes the Boss! Does this mean that the Christian will have no virtuous deeds, good works, in his life? Certainly not. It means that what one does after surrender is done at the Lord's bidding, and thus "works" are the result of true faith. It means that the fruits of the Spirit are the Spirit's fruits, not the believer's fruits. They are as much a gift of grace as are justification and salvation.

The role and purpose of the gospel message is to convert men and women to the Lord, who offers a life of victory through divine aid. When Christ first confronts the sinner, the sinner must make an initial surrender. Then there follows daily surrender to Him throughout life. When the pastor realizes man's need for surrender and conversion, he will find that his preaching must take that need into account.

FOCUS ON PREACHING

Preaching became one of my most important tasks as an evangelical minister, if not the most important. We are living in a perishing world, a fact obvious to every serious-minded and Biblically alert Christian. No human institution is capable of resolving the world's grave and threatening problems. While the history of mankind reflects marvelous progress in technology and science, it also reveals complete moral failure in human relationships. Many pessimistic leaders in the secular world today see no hope of solving its tensions, perhaps not even maintaining the *status quo*. Now is precisely the time for the Christian realist to make his mark. It is a time when those called by God to preach and teach His Word must know the message of the Bible clearly and proclaim it with boldness, assurance, and clarity.

Inspiration designed the message of the Bible to transform human life and character. It is not merely a compilation of interesting and provocative religious information. Information is only for the mind, the intellect. But God wants to reach the heart of man with the Gospel of forgiveness and hope. Certainly the mind is involved because a person must understand, and the will comes into the picture because he must make a decision on the basis of that understanding, but with the heart, the emotions, he responds in love to the God who calls through the gospel. Therefore the preacher must appeal to the mind, the heart, and the will. His message must be Christ-centered, rooted in the

Bible, and must meet the inner need for forgiveness and hope. It must always call, either explicitly or implicitly, for a decision on the part of the hearer. Every time the gospel is heard the hearer must make a decision for or against it, to either obey or disobey. The Holy Spirit works on the conscience, for no one can listen to the Word of God for long without taking some kind of action. Either he will leave the church so as not to hear it any longer, hardening his heart in stubborn rebellion against what he knows to be truth, or surrender to it and find salvation. The ultimate outcome of revelation is transformation of human life not just increased information for the mind.

People need to know God, and the preacher must make an appeal, as did the Apostle Paul, and say, "We beseech you on behalf of Christ, be reconciled to God." (2 Cor. 5:20) Never in the history of Christianity has Paul's counsel to Timothy been more relevant for the ministry:

> *I charge you in the presence of God and of Christ Jesus who is to judge the living and the dead, and by his appearing and his kingdom: preach the word, be urgent in season and out of season, convince, rebuke, and exhort, be unfailing in patience and in teaching. For the time is coming when people will not endure sound teaching, but having itching ears they will accumulate for themselves teachers to suit their own likings, and will turn away from listening to the truth and wander into myths. As for you, always be steady, endure suffering, do the work of an evangelist, fulfil your ministry. (2 Tim. 4:1-5)*

Paul's counsel to preachers appears in the framework of last-day events. Because Christ will soon return to claim His faithful Church and to execute judgment, the call to repentance and faith in Him must go forth despite all opposition. Paul clearly pictures the Church of our day. On the theological level we see a definite departure from the Bible. On the parish level this results in humanist and secular views creeping into religious education. Questions are raised that create doubt and few answers from the Bible are given that stimulate faith.

The individual church member who wants to be religious while still indulging the appetites of the flesh often accepts such anti-Biblical trends. Many church members wish to be left undisturbed in their comfortable delusions and misconceptions. The preacher who insists on preaching and teaching righteousness by grace through faith in Christ as opposed to the subtle religious-works righteousness prevalent today will not win any popularity contests. Many congregations prefer ministers whose preaching does not challenge their delusions, does not urge them to repentance, to faith, or surrender to Jesus Christ. Like sheep without a shepherd, they wander in the forest of myth, philosophy, and religiosity and become eternally lost while maintaining a facade of Christianity.

EVANGELISM

It was only natural that my beliefs about the role and function of preaching should affect both my approach to the ministry and my methods. I have never agreed with the view that a person was a Christian simply because he was baptized, held church membership, attended communion regularly, and contributed liberally. Such a view is pure legalism. The preacher must never take for granted that the parishioners are all Christians. If he did, he would never make an appeal to the lost. On the other hand, it must not be assumed that no one is Christian. Then sermons would never be preached designed to encourage growth in sanctification. Rather, the gospel must be presented in such a way as to touch the hearts of unconverted and converted alike.

Early in my ministry I began to preach evangelistically. I do not mean that every sermon ended with an altar call, an explicit call for decisions. But I did my best to clearly expose the teaching of the text so that the listeners might know where they stood and what God was calling them to do. At the same time I would impress them with the necessity to choose, because people need to make religious decisions.

Together with my own preaching and teaching, I believed it essential to have at least one special evangelistic series each year. My first parish welcomed enthusiastically such meetings, as the people were accustomed to the Biblical and evangelistic emphasis vital to the Finnish Evangelical Lutheran Church. I can think of a number of individuals who were touched by the Spirit during such evangelistic meetings, in particular a young boy who was healed of rheumatic fever, and many others who accepted Christ or experienced awakening and revival.

21

For two and a half years I served that parish of three congregations. The people were kind and responsive to the ministry of a young pastor still "wet behind the ears." It seemed, however, that I spent more time driving--32,000 miles a year--than in studying and ministering. When the opportunity came to move to another parish of one congregation of approximately six hundred members, I readily accepted. Eagerly received by the new congregation, as having a young pastor for a change overjoyed them, I began my ministry at Sharon Lutheran Church in Bessemer, Michigan.

During the initial interview with the church board we discussed at length the needs of the parish. They had a particular concern for the youth. When I asked their opinions regarding the preaching ministry of their pastor they had but one request, that I preach sermons they could understand! I assured them that I would always have the congregation's spiritual needs uppermost in my mind.

Realizing the difference in background between the new parish and the previous one, I knew I must proceed with caution relative to evangelism. First, I had to build their confidence in myself as their pastor. My initial goal was to preach sermons that touched the heart and built faith; sermons that would make them sensitive to their need for a deeper spiritual experience with Christ. I visited the members in their homes, praying with them, as well as those who were hospitalized, and focused on developing rapport with the congregation. After two years of that kind of pastoral concern I felt the time had come to move forward into evangelism.

The congregation agreed to a special series of meetings designed to introduce them gently to evangelistic outreach. The first series was composed of Bible lectures, rather than the traditional type of evangelistic meeting. For a week we had evening meetings for adults and morning Bible study breakfasts for the youth on their way to school. Both morning and evening our guest speaker, a well-known Lutheran Bible teacher from the Lutheran Bible Institute of Minneapolis, simply taught from a New Testament epistle.

Hoping that my people would respond more positively to evangelism if they knew and trusted the evangelist, I suggested that they invite my brother-in-law, a fellow Lutheran pastor, for a fall evangelistic campaign. the response was positive, and the following year we obtained the services of a professional Lutheran evangelist from the Lutheran Evangelistic Movement in Minneapolis. Such meetings continued for two more years. They led to some outright conversions, and revived and restored the faith of others. The Holy Spirit was at work! It thrilled me to see a number of dear people open their minds and hearts more fully to Jesus Christ. I rejoiced when some began to exercise their redeemed wills and apply the teachings of the Bible in their daily lives. It was an exciting time in ministry!

NEW LIFE SINGERS

As I gradually focused on the youth, praying for them and relating to them in a more personal way, they began to respond to Christ's appeal. A concept of youth-to-youth ministry began to develop in their minds. I will never forget the evening that three of them asked me if they could form a youth gospel team. Of course I encouraged them and two weeks later they invited me to hear them. In amazement I sat spellbound, as they presented their witness in song, with piano and guitar accompaniment. I could hardly contain my excitement as the group's potential gripped me. They had put together a gospel program designed to reach youth with the relevancy of the Christian faith. That night a fresh breeze began to blow in the congregation. Overjoyed at my enthusiastic response, those vibrant young people crowded around me and promised to polish their presentation. I, in turn, vowed to arrange opportunities for them to share it.

The next year was an exciting one for them, and for me. Adopting the name *NEW LIFE SINGERS*, and uniformed in red and white, they traveled to many churches in Michigan's Upper Peninsula. Their program produced an immediate impact and many invitations came. Their adult counselors and I, soon realized that the group needed a bus. In the face of some determined opposition, the congregation became the somewhat reluctant owner of a ten-year old school bus. Promptly named "Joshua" by the young people, because Biblical Joshua made it to the promised land, it took them on many trips to youth rallies, to Bible camps in the summers, and an unforgettable trip to Duluth, Minnesota for a television appearance.

"Joshua" made possible many decisions for Christ one summer as "he" faithfully hauled a busload to Bible camp. Many people were praying that by the time they returned home, every youth on board would come to know Jesus Christ in a personal way. It happened! Night after night two or three of them responded to the evangelist's altar call until every one made a personal decision for Christ. Their singing during the trip home to Bessemer in faithful "Joshua" was something to remember! Their youthful eagerness to share Christ, and their boldness in doing so were infectious. Throughout my entire ministry I will never regret what was required in order to override opposition to the ministry of those thirty-plus young believers.

Many adults in the congregation began to see the need for a more personal, as opposed to a cultural, faith as well as more openness in sharing it. Almost spontaneously a fellowship group formed to meet biweekly in various homes. They discussed the Bible, shared spiritual insights and blessings as well as personal struggles. They were learning that faith is the struggle to be believing. They came to know and accept each other as individual believers, spiritual pilgrims and disciples of Christ, and their developing Christian love for each other brought joy to my heart. As time went on those biweekly fellowship gatherings became a vital part of their, and my, Christian experience. They were sacred "social meetings" in the finest pietistic tradition.

In connection with the growing desire among the members to witness and testify to others, I began to focus more on sanctification and spiritual growth in my sermons and in the various Sunday School classes and on other occassions.

Many members received a new vision, new insight into the reality and nature of the Christian faith and life. I loved all my people and felt confident that in time they would all see what God had in mind for them. As we would continue to pray and work, preach the Word of God week after week, the fruits of the Spirit would surely increase. My congregation was one of the most active in the area. For six happy years I worked in their midst, motivating them as best I could to a deeper faith and a wider ministry in the community. God blessed our work together and the Holy Spirit touched some people with conversion, others with awakening and revival. Youth caught a vision of what Christ could do for them and with them.

Daily I sought the Lord for wisdom and strength in ministering to my people, and for those who came to me for counsel. I discovered that when I was faithful in preaching what the Bible says, with no compromise, there would be individuals needing spiritual soul care and coming to me for help. With my ministry being blessed in spite of my own weaknesses, I remembered the Biblical promise that God uses the weak things of the world to confound the strong.

It was in the midst of that most satisfying and fruitful ministry that I faced the greatest spiritual crisis in my Christian life.

4

THE STRANGER IN MY HOME

It was quite a shock, after fourteen years of marriage, to find myself living with a stranger. For fourteen years we had built our marriage and were thankful for the understanding and the compatibility we achieved. As with all marriages, ours had its difficult moments, but, confident of God's love and care, we made them stepping stones rather than stumbling blocks. Our happiest years were those in Bessemer, Michigan, and the church members respected and admired Shirley for her witness for Christ.

SPIRITUAL VITALITY

Shirley has always been extremely serious about living for Christ and often expresses the belief that the Christian woman must totally devote herself to the Lord. She sought to put that into practice in her relationship with family, friends, church, and community. Serious Bible study was always a vital part of her life, and continues to be. Her love for the Bible as God's Word is deep and abiding. She trusts its counsel as life's only safe and reliable guide. Sunday School, Bible camps, and, of special importance, the reverence with which her parents held the Bible fostered her faith and trust in the written Word of God.

Very active in the Luther League youth organization, she loved the church and all of the activities related to the life of a busy parish. When she graduated from high school, she naturally thought of enrolling in a Christian college and attended Suomi College during the academic year 1950-51. While there she appreciated and enjoyed immensely the spiritual emphasis and took part in dormitory devotionals, prayer meetings, and trips with other students to various area churches.

EXERCISE AND THE ADVENTISTS

Coupled with her spiritual vitality was always a love for sports. Swimming, bicycling, tennis, ice-skating, and skiing comprise only a few of the physical activities she does well. Her lively and enthusiastic interest in sports is not confined solely to their enjoyment for their own sake. They are a necessity. Constitutionally, she is the kind of person whose entire emotional, psychological, mental, and spiritual well-being is directly connected with her physical health. Her spirits rise and life seems most positive and victorious when she exercises.

Shirley was always searching for someone who felt the same way about sports and exercise, someone who shared her instinctive understanding that physical well-being and spiritual well-being are interrelated. Then she met another Christian who had the same outlook. She learned of a Lutheran lady who had set up a basketball hoop in an old barn for the youth of the neighborhood and asked if she could join in the games. During one of the games the Lutheran lady introduced her to the wife of the Seventh-day Adventist dentist for whom she worked. Learning that Shirley loved sports, *Bert* (Bertha) Bigford invited her to join the Adventists in their periodic volleyball games which they played in a local gymnasium. Happy to join them, Shirley discovered people who felt as she did about the essential nature of wholesome activity and exercise.

Soon the two became close friends. In the summer they often played tennis, and skated and skiied together in the winter. Volleyball and swimming also formed a part of their yearly round of exercise.

Directly related to Shirley's need for physical exercise was a rather severe battle with colitis. Our family doctor, who was a Seventh-day Adventist, emphatically prescribed exercise. She decided on bicycle riding. With grim determination she began to develop the leg and lung capacity for long rides. Soon she made a daily ten mile round trip to the next town. By the end of the summer the colitis was gone. That experience deepened her conviction of the need for vigorous physical activity. Naturally, she urged many of her acquaintances to adopt a program of daily exercise.

28

During the same period she made the discovery that her diet had a direct bearing on both physical and spiritual health. A long struggle with insomnia ended when she decided to forsake coffee. That was a difficult victory as coffee was almost like "holy water" to the Finnish people. No church social could be held without the serving of coffee.

I encouraged Shirley in her exercise program as the children and I were the beneficiaries of her good health. She was the happiest, the most content, and the most eager and conscientious wife and mother when she felt in tune with God and nature. She wanted to know and experience the best possible life that God had in mind for her and was willing to discipline herself to that end.

CHRISTIAN LIFESTYLE

The Bible counsels the Christian to practice self-control. (Romans 8:6; 13:14; Galatians 5:16, 19; Philippians 3:3.) The Reformation and the Lutheran pietistic tradition have also stressed it. Responding to her pietistic Lutheran upbringing, Shirley, early in her life, adopted high standards of Christian behavior and morality. She would not participate in dances, nor would she use tobacco or alcoholic beverages. She adopted a simple but becoming style of dress which reflected her basic modesty, and never used excessive makeup or adornments. Her hair style, for many years, has been a simple braid.[1]

Because I know her better than anyone else, I can attest to the fact that while she adopted these principles for herself, she does not feel superior to others, nor does she condemn those who choose to live differently. The standards she imposes upon herself are high because they are not her own. She has believed them to be God's will for Christian living as revealed in the Bible.

Shirley's love for evangelical, orthodox Lutheranism was apparent. She expressed that love in many tangible ways, such as her early decision to tithe her income in support of the church's mission in the world. Her favorite beneficiaries were evangelistic in nature, such as the Lutheran Hour and the Lutheran Evangelistic Movement (LEM). She was always

------

[1] She explains the reasons for choosing the braid in her book *No Turning Back*, POINTER Publications, 1988.

grateful, and continues to be, for the Lutheran heritage that has molded her spiritual life. The evangelical and pietistic Lutheranism of Finland embodied in her a love for the Bible as the Word of God, a strong sense of world mission, and an urgent concern for the salvation of mankind. All through our married life she has been a stable spiritual force and influence.

ADVENTIST CAMP MEETING

With a new friend who took the Christian faith as seriously as she did, Shirley began to share that faith with *Bert*. They discussed the Bible and prayed together. As their friendship deepened, Shirley felt a growing conviction that her new friend might, somehow, be part of God's continually unfolding plan for her life. When *Bert* invited her to attend a Seventh-day Adventist camp meeting in Wisconsin, she accepted. Curiosity and the need for spiritual fellowship prompted her decision. She loved Bible camp, and hardly a summer passed by without her spending at least one week at a Bible camp. The Christian fellowship and deep Bible study were almost as essential for her as exercise.

During that camp meeting she heard a study of the Gospel of John, which proclaimed and emphasized Christ. Visiting with the speaker later, she discovered that he had spent a year at a Lutheran theological seminary. His quotation of the verse "Be faithful unto death, and I will give you the crown of life" (Revelation 2:10) represented further indication to her that God was indeed leading in the decision to come to the camp meeting. The speaker reminded her of a saintly Lutheran evangelist she knew and respected.

The evening speaker, who was the prominent Adventist evangelist Joe Crews, also created a favorable impression as he revealed the unity and harmony of the Adventist message and showed from the Bible how God had raised up and will use the Adventist movement in His divine plan. Shirley began to see importance in the Sabbath and its connection with God's plan for earth's last days. An evening service repeated His warning to Lot and his wife, "Look not behind thee." Immediately she thought of the radio sermon on the same theme which had seemed to come in answer to her prayers a few days before.

The following day Shirley met a kindly woman who inquired whether she was a Seventh-day Adventist. When she answered no, the woman related how she felt strongly impressed to pray for her the moment she first saw her on the campgrounds.

On another occasion Shirley heard a man and his wife relate in a captivating manner the factors behind their decision to join the Adventist Church after life-long membership in the Lutheran Church. Speaking to them later, she received their promise of prayer. Their sincerity and genuine witness for Christ was impressive.

The daily meetings and personal contacts intensified Shirley's interest. She began to listen with greater concentration. It became vital not to miss a single word. She sensed that the future might depend on what she heard. She told me later of her excitement, but also her fear of facing the implications and consequences of what she heard.

She spent much time praying during that week, earnestly asking for God's guidance. She recognized truth in what she heard, as she tested it with Scripture. At the end of the week she responded to an altar call and requested special prayer. Her need for guidance and direction from the Lord was acute as her conscience became captive to what was taught from the Word of God.

At that Adventist camp meeting she observed her first seventh-day Sabbath and vowed to keep that day holy as part of her faith response to Christ for the rest of her life.

MOUNTING TENSION

Great difficulties, she knew, would face her when she got back home. She would return to a husband who was a Lutheran minister, and to the life of a Lutheran parsonage. Her responsibilities as the pastor's wife awaited her. Any religiously divided home is bad enough, but a divided minister's home would present special problems. She had many individuals to consider during the drive back home to Bessemer. Her two children, her pastor husband, her brother who had been a Lutheran pastor for twenty years, another brother who was a lay preacher, other members of her family and mine, and all the members of the congregation. Her new convictions would have serious effects and consequences in the lives of all of them. Yet she also knew that she must follow the way God seemed to be leading.

Wanting to remain honest and forthright and to keep nothing secret, she determined to share it all with me as

31

soon as she got back home. Unfortunately an opportune time did not present itself prior to the incident described in chapter one.

Shirley's only decision up to that unhappy Saturday was to observe the Sabbath. She had not yet chosen to join the Adventist Church, although I feared it would become inevitable.

However, as she continued to read and study, she began to practice more and more of their teachings. Her lifestyle radically changed as she began observing the seventh-day Sabbath and following many of the health principles Adventists advocate.

At the time I could not see the relationship between her past convictions and life-style and that which she had begun to practice. It only seemed so radically different in spite of her previous conservatism. With everyone we knew worshipping on Sunday, she observed Saturday as the holy day. With all her family and friends lovers of well-cooked and seasoned meat, and proficient in its preparation herself, she adopted a meatless diet. With no one we knew seeing anything amiss in the moderate wearing of jewelry, she elected to put it aside completely including her wedding band and engagement ring. In spite of the assurance that her decision in no way represented a change in our personal relationship, it was, nevertheless, the behavior of a stranger as far as I was concerned.

As the days went sadly by and my perplexity increased, the trauma dominated my thoughts and seriously impaired our relationship. Almost unbearable strain and tension replaced the normal relaxation and peace in our home. Discord replaced harmony. It was impossible to shield the children. Communication became more and more difficult, and I became as much a stranger to her as she was to me.

5

A SAD SUNDAY

I refused to listen to anything Shirley wanted to say. As far as I was concerned, her ideas were foolishness and had more to do with friendship than with truth.

Now I see that I was as much responsible for the strain and tension as she. Over the years we had developed the practice of sharing our thoughts and feelings openly and freely, especially those involving faith and God's direction in our lives. Shirley had counted on that practice to tell me of her new convictions and how she believed God to be directing her decision. But I wouldn't listen! The shock was too great. I had no desire to understand.

THREAT TO MY MINISTRY

After dismissing the baby-sitter on that fateful Saturday, I began to plead, argue, cajole, and ridicule, as well as demand that she put all thought of Adventism out of her mind. I had only a limited knowledge of Seventh-day Adventist doctrine, but felt certain of its heretical nature. I was certain it represented legalism and a radical departure from historic Christianity.

As far as the Sabbath was concerned, I taught the fourth commandment yearly to my catechetical classes believing in the principle of the Sabbath but not its seventh-day observance. It did not apply to the Christian Church. With her long Lutheran training, and its emphasis on the grace of God, I could not see how Shirley could accept any other point of view. As a result I concluded that it must be her friendship with *Bert* Bigford that was the real cause of it all.

The threat to my ministry was so acute I was willing to cast aside all previous trust in Shirley's spiritual judgment. I bluntly expressed my belief that she was sick, which, of course, was terrible for her to hear from me.

How she could change so radically in only ten days I could not comprehend. Just a few weeks earlier I gave her theological "ammunition" to refute her friend over the telephone. I felt very confident and certain of her evangelical faith. But everything had changed.

A DESPERATE TRIP

My anguish grew and all I could think of was to get Shirley to her pastor brother. Fast! Since I could not convince her to reject Adventism, perhaps he could. I called him on the phone, haltingly explained the situation, and asked if we would be welcome for a visit. He urged us to come. Fortunately, it was vacation time and we left the very next day for Port Arthur, Canada.

The drive there was tense. A heavy and oppressive silence alternated with my argumentative attempts to change her mind. By then Shirley knew I would not listen to her side of the story at all, and she decided that silence was the better part of wisdom. Her silence then, and later, infuriated me. I interpreted it as pure stubbornness, and a refusal to listen to and follow my advice. She just didn't care, I thought.

At the first opportunity, after we arrived, I began to explain the situation to Shirley's brother. She valued his spiritual counsel and would surely, I desperately hoped, heed him at such a crucial moment in our lives. He, too, seemed to think that Shirley's friendship with Mrs. Bigford was the primary factor.

We spent a week touring the area, picnicking, swimming, boating. Her brother arranged for the use of a lake cottage for two days. The cool weather forced us to spend most of the time indoors. I discovered that Shirley had filled her suitcase with Adventist books and pamphlets, which she read every spare moment. The days went by, and her brother said nothing to her. Growing more anxious, I pleaded with him to speak to her. He felt, however, that the best approach was to let her work it out for herself. Opposition would only drive her further on.

After a week we went home. I felt the trip was a failure, had accomplished little, and only given Shirley the idea that her brother did not disapprove. My burden felt even greater when we arrived back in my parish with nothing resolved.

Her brother had given me a book to read, however, and suggested that perhaps Shirley would want to look it over too. It absorbed my attention for many days. The author accepted the Adventist Church as Christian but attempted to refute its doctrines of the Sabbath, the ministry of Christ in a heavenly sanctuary, and the pre-second Advent judgment. I tried to use his arguments to persuade Shirley that she was on dangerous ground. What she was getting into would not satisfy her, I said, as it would only draw her away from Christ rather than enhance her relationship to Him. I begged her to read the book, but she would not.

Shirley spent most of her leisure time reading all the Adventist publications she could find. Her friend and the local Adventist congregation kept her well supplied. I found those books, tracts, and pamphlets all over the house. Books written by Ellen G. White particularly absorbed her attention. Gradually I came to detest the sight of them as they were the symbols of my anguish.

Her refusal to read the book her brother gave me, plus some other material I had received, as well as her absorbing interest in books by Ellen G. White, irritated me. Sometimes I would yank a book from her hands and hurl it violently across the room. If the book was damaged, I rejoiced. They were part of the cause for the most threatening and agonizing experience of my life.

BOOK BURNING

As my frustration and fear increased, my anger grew more violent. With no sign of help coming from anywhere, my prayer life became barren of hope. God was not listening, I concluded. I thought only of lashing out furiously at the thing threatening my ministry and my family. My hostility forced Shirley to read in secret while I was away from the house, or where she could quickly dispose of the book should she hear me coming. One favorite hiding place was in the clothes hamper underneath the soiled garments.

Though the situation was fraught with anguish and pain, it was not without humorous moments. One day Shirley was seated on the bed reading when Mrs. Bigford came by to take her shopping. Later at the supermarket she suddenly gasped, "Oh, my goodness! I've left Mrs. White under the bed!"

Always searching the house for the hated books, one day to my great joy I discovered a cache. With even greater pleasure I filled a grocery bag, drove to the garbage dump, and venting my mounting frustration pitched the books gleefully into the fire and smoke. To my satisfaction the flames curled over *Dimensions In Salvation*, scorched it black, and devoured it. After that Mrs. Bigford safely kept Shirley's books except for one or two she was currently reading.

Years later I met the author of that book, W. R. Beach, and told him the story of its burning. He felt highly complimented. Today I consider it to be one of the most outstanding and articulate presentations of the Adventist faith.

Deeply worried about Shirley's salvation, I saw her new life-style as pure legalism and believed that in the end it would destroy her profound relationship with Christ. Fearful that she was adopting a philosophy of works-righteousness, I tried to help her see her error.

The thought whirled around in my mind that if she persisted in her beliefs, it would destroy the future of my ministry. My fearful reaction to that thought nearly destroyed me physically and spiritually. Self-pity dominated as I imagined all my hopes and dreams for future service in the church dashed to pieces.

Because I considered some of the doctrines of Adventism heretical, I foresaw great conflict looming ahead in the religious training of our children.

Prejudice and bitterness possessed me as I permitted hatred for Dr. and Mrs. Bigford and all Seventh-day Adventists to lodge in my heart. Words fail to describe the inner devastation and desolation, the feeling of being powerless in defending my family against what I considered to be satanic. I forbade Mrs. Bigford to set foot in my house and, while I knew I could not ultimately control her movements, ordered Shirley not to visit her anymore.

My mental anguish and frustration caused me to think and do things I never thought I could or would do. I shouted. I pounded on the table and walls. I cursed. Long forgotten words flew unbidden to my lips. Worst of all, I struck my wife for the first and only time in our relationship. Daily I fought the desire to lash out at those who I felt had interfered in my life.

In desperation I went to three clergymen friends for help and counsel. All three were convinced that the situation constituted a satanic attack on my ministry. They believed I must give Shirley an ultimatum. She must choose between her family and the Adventist Church.

Desperately I sought to understand what God's purpose might be in allowing these events, but the bitterness in my heart had all but destroyed the channel of communication with Him. Almost daily I demanded how He could allow such a thing to happen to us. He was revealing a face I had never seen before. How could He permit a situation where I must choose between wife and ministry, both of which I had accepted as His gift? The agony grew unbearable.

Much preferring to believe my wife mentally ill than an instrument of Satan, I urged her to submit to a psychological examination. My lack of trust and confidence in her spiritual knowledge and discernment disappointed her intensely. But I was catching at straws in a desperate attempt to find a solution to an impossible dilemma. She refused to have the tests, pleading with me to listen to her story. I would have none of it. She must forsake Adventism or else, I threatened time and time again.

HOSTILITY RESOLVED

Gradually I began to consider following the advice of my three friends and suffered terribly with the thought. Faced with the prospect of presenting Shirley with an ultimatum, I found my health deteriorating. My appetite virtually vanished. It became increasingly more difficult to sleep, and I would wake up suddenly in the night. My mind dwelt obsessively on my problem, and I would frequently wander around the darkened house. Casting about for a solution, I began to work up the courage to face my wife with a choice between her family and Adventism. Daily I became more agitated and found it more difficult to concentrate on my ministry. My sermons deteriorated. Unknowingly they reflected my anguish. Only my three friends, Shirley's two brothers, and one other friend knew the actual nature of the dilemma, however.

Returning home one day from calling on sick parishioners in the hospital, I suddenly knew what I must do. It was like a flash of illumination. I remembered the experience of Job and realized that I, too, could not accept the counsel of my three friends. Instead, I had to do what my conscience told me was right as a Christian husband and father. I had pledged myself to Shirley for life, for better or for worse. That vow was made prior to my ordination vow. It took precedence. It must be honored. The advice of my friends was wrong. My heart sang as I literally felt an immense weight lifted from my shoulders. The rest of the way home I sang out loud in joy and thankfulness.

When I told Shirley what had happened, a tremendous load was lifted from her mind as well. She had lived in dread of being forced to choose between her marriage and her religion.

With that particular burden gone, I took up my work again with some degree of stability and hope.

However, another problem weighed upon my heart, my hatred for Dr. and Mrs. Bigford. My physical condition still failed to improve, I believed, because of the hate I carried. I knew it was wrong. A Christian cannot live with hatred without it destroying his soul, his very life. Looking back, I believe that if my extreme hostility had not been resolved I would have lost my relationship with Christ and been physically and spiritually ruined.

One day I stood in the aisle of the empty church and related to God the whole sordid tale. I told Him of my hatred and bitterness and the reasons for it. I told Him what agony I felt, yet how I realized the hatred was opposed to His pattern of life. Then, before the altar, where so often I had given and received the Lord's Supper, I prostrated myself in repentance and confession, begging for His mercy and forgiveness. I was determined not to rise until He blessed me! What a joy to know a God who freely forgives! Again I felt a burden lifted. Before leaving the sanctuary, I prayed for the courage to confess my hatred to the Bigford's and ask them to forgive me.

It was not easy to beg the forgiveness of someone whose beliefs had caused me so much anguish. I could not have done it without the help of my Lord and His Holy Spirit. Of course the Bigfords quickly forgave and we have been friends ever since.

From that moment on I was free to consider the situation in a more objective fashion, and seriously inquire of God what His purpose and will might be. To be sure, ups and downs, regressions and recriminations, still came, but the overall focus was much more positive and hopeful. I clung to the Bible verse, a Word of power from God, that sustained me through it all:

For I know the plans I have for you, says the Lord, plans for welfare and not for evil, to give you a future and a hope. (Jeremiah 29:11)

Hope I desperately needed. But what about the future? What would it hold?

TRIP TO FINLAND

Shirley and I began to plan for a long-awaited vacation trip to Europe and Finland during the spring and summer of 1969. We invited the Bigfords to go with us. The trip would last seven weeks. We left our two children with trusted friends and departed in late May. The Bigfords came two weeks later and we met in Luxembourg. We drove up the Rhine River, then north to Denmark, Sweden, and finally to Finland, where the Bigfords departed for home from Helsinki. The next two weeks Shirley and I visited relatives and friends.

Throughout the trip I hoped that perhaps visiting the birthplaces of her parents might gently persuade Shirley to return to Lutheranism. We worshipped in the church where her mother was confirmed as a young girl. The present tenants of her old home invited us in to see it, which was an emotional experience for Shirley. In Helsinki, on our last Sunday in Finland, we attended the service at the "Old Church," (*vanha kirko*). It was communion Sunday, and together we knelt at the old historic communion rail to receive the Lord's Supper--the last time, as events would prove, that we communed together as Lutheran believers. Somehow it was fitting that it took place there.

SHIRLEY JOINS THE ADVENTIST CHURCH

Although it was a memorable vacation, it failed to reverse Shirley's convictions. Back in the United States, she

39

went again to camp meeting, more receptive to Seventh-day Adventist teaching than ever, and more determined as to their soundness. After camp meeting she informed me of her decision--she felt she must join the Seventh-day Adventist Church. Her baptism would take place on September 6, 1969.

August 31, 1969, was a sad Sunday. I had the unhappy duty of announcing her decision to the congregation of Sharon Lutheran Church.

"This is the first time in eight years of ministry that I cannot preach," I began. Then continued:

I have no sermon for you today. . . It is the saddest and most difficult day of my life. . . I must inform you that next Saturday my wife is severing her relationship with the Lutheran Church that has nurtured her faith for thirty-seven years, in order to become a part of the Seventh-day Adventist movement. I wanted to make this announcement myself rather than have you hear about it by word of mouth.

I told my people that the size of my burden left little room for anyone else's. Up until then I had hoped she would be persuaded to change her mind. As for Adventism, I believed it to be "a part of the false teachings--false prophets of the end times." I expressed my hope and wish "to continue serving my Lord in the Lutheran ministry." In addition, I pleaded for my congregation's support, understanding, and willingness to forgive Shirley. And for their prayers for us all. Only their prayers could sustain me in the weeks, months, and years ahead.

Reaffirming my love for Shirley, I called on them to love her too. It would not be easy, but it was not easy for God to love us either. It cost the blood of His Son.

At my insistence Shirley bravely sat through it all, in a front pew with our children, publicly acknowledging her decision. I asked her to stand with me following the service to greet the congregation. I felt that if she had the courage to do this she should also have the courage to answer for it. Responses and reactions were varied. To say that the people were shocked is to put it mildly.

Many members tearfully shook her hand as she stood beside me. Some embraced her and assured her of their love. Many could not speak, only grip her hand tightly. A few wished her well. Others expressed the hope that one day she would return. A few would not speak to her and revealed understandable anger, disappointment, and deep hurt.

To me they expressed their sorrow and regret, as well as their profound sympathy, and pledged their prayers. Many did not understand what was happening and never would.

My heart was sad for them, for we, whom God had called to bring them hope and peace in Christ, had become the cause of pain and suffering. Many of them did not know what to do or say. They were numb.

Shirley actively joined the Seventh-day Adventist congregation in Ironwood, Michigan, a larger town west of Bessemer. Though she attended the Sabbath services there each Saturday, she was also equally faithful in sitting with our children during the Sunday services in the church I pastored. That arrangement continued for the next year until we left Bessemer, since I would not permit our children to attend the Adventist church.

After that sad Sunday I felt completely alone in my ministry. The wife who so faithfully supported me through seven years of education and nine years of ministry, was a stranger.

6

CRISIS AND ITS CONSEQUENCES

Accepting the fact that Shirley was going to join the Seventh-day Adventist Church was a long, difficult process. In a way that process began on a pine-covered hilltop in Finland. There, alone, I pondered the future. Doubts flooded my feverish mind. Gazing to the south, I saw the last golden rays of the setting sun striking the ornate gable and bell tower of the ancient church of Porvoo, a building which had played so vital a role in the history of that land of my ancestors. As the sun set and the church slowly blended into its surroundings, my spirits darkened also. Small lights began to flicker in the cottage windows of the old town below, and the small river sparkled anew with reflected light. Were those lights in the darkness promises of the light I would later see in my own darkness?

WRESTLING WITH GOD

That night on a hill so far from home I wrestled with God and with doubt. My faith in Him had reached its lowest point. As evening darkness swallowed the beautiful old church, it seemed as though my heart was being sucked into a horribly unmerciful gloom.

Returning to the tourist campground, I wrote a letter to my brother-in-law, which, fortunately, I never sent:

I don't know what I am going to do when I get back. God is not answering my prayers, and I have given it up as a lost cause. It seems that I must make some kind of decision when I get back. I don't know what to do. I'm being literally torn apart inside by the

contest between faithfulness as a husband and faithful-
ness as an evangelical preacher. This has caused a
severe (I use the word strongly) strain upon my faith,
and I now have doubts crowding into my mind as to the
validity of the Bible, the reality of God, and even of
the experience of the past fourteen years. I feel
forsaken by both God and wife. I dread our homecom-
ing. The thought of facing my congregation and of
preparing sermons again terrifies me. We shall just
have to wait and see what homecoming brings about.
As it is now, I just cannot see myself continuing in the
ministry any longer--my heart seems to have gone out
of it all, and I am deeply, perhaps hopelessly, depressed.

With every intention of mailing the letter at the first opportunity, I sealed it. But God does not forsake one of His own. My doubts were real, but God sustained my flickering faith and fanned it into flame once again. With the small faith that remained, I gave Him no rest, daily reminding Him of His promise to give me a future and a hope. Slowly I began to believe again that He would do what He promised. How could I disbelieve Him and deny Him when He had repeatedly proven His trustworthiness in the past? There in Finland I began to wonder if perhaps God was dealing with me just as He had in the past, and I simply did not yet recognize the fact. Perhaps He was arranging circumstances in such a way that I could sense His leading. After I was able to reaffirm belief that God was on my side and would not forsake me, it was possible to adopt a more positive outlook.

While I still felt apprehensive about returning to my parish, I did look forward to preaching again. How God would lead and resolve my dilemma, I had no way of knowing. All I knew was that He would.

With faith renewing, I was even able to face the possibility of Shirley's membership in the Seventh-day Adventist Church. Only by divine aid did I manage to pick up the threads of my ministry and carry on.

With confidence in my Lord's love and care growing firm once again, the future began to beckon with promise. To be sure, I knew I had yet to face difficult moments, but I felt I could deal with them confidently. "Pray that you might know what God is saying to you," a former teacher and trusted friend said to me. When my other three friends were giving me advice I could not ultimately follow, he offered me positive and helpful counsel. Spiritual counsel. He was not just a theologian, he was a deeply spiritual man who knew God. Never judgmental or condemnatory toward Shirley's new beliefs and decision, he pledged his love and friendship to both of us and promised to pray for us each day. What more could one ask of a friend?

HOME AGAIN

During the fall of 1969 I conducted another series of evangelistic meetings and the Holy Spirit touched lives anew. A religious fellowship group spontaneously formed as a consequence of the meetings, and as spiritual hunger became acute.

Designed to informally strengthen and nurture faith as well as serve as an opportunity for deeper Bible study, that fellowship group became an important source of encouragement to me. The biweekly meetings were open to the whole congregation and announced in the weekly bulletin. I needed the assurance and hope that came from sharing sorrow and joy. The members of that group will probably never know how important they were to me, how their friendship and Christian ministry to their pastor kept me going.

The ministry of the *New Life Singers*, the youth gospel team, was in full swing that fall. That, too, was a marvelous source of inspiration. Unforgettable was the trip to Duluth, Minnesota, for an appearance on the Dotty Becker Show. Traveling with those wonderful young people will ever remain a fond and treasured memory. Their openness to the love of God in Christ, their vision of youth-to-youth ministry and evangelism, their total lack of prejudice, and their eagerness to accept one another will long remain a source of inspiration to me. When I left Bessemer, they presented me with a bronze cross inscribed "New Life Singers--A Cross of Love." It now hangs just behind my head in my office at the Seventh-day Adventist Theological Seminary. It is the first thing I see when I enter my office to begin the day, and never fails to remind me of my Lord's sacrifice for my salvation and of their love for their pastor/friend.

My congregation of earnest and sincere people supported me fully through the years as their pastor, contributing faithfully to the church's budget. During the first year of my pastorate the congregation constructed an educational building, installed a new heating plant for both buildings, and made some badly needed renovations in the sanctuary. Through excellent stewardship they liquidated the debt by the late fall of 1970. On a recent vacation trip I worshipped with them once again and *Kastman Hall*, the educational facility, still looks like new.

Over the years, worship attendance gradually increased until the crisis in 1969. Understandably, it then dropped alarmingly as the unpleasant situation confused and distressed many members. It was not easy for the congregation to accept the pastor's wife joining another denomination. You can, I'm sure, imagine the kind of feelings it aroused. Shirley's decision called into question not only everything I believed and stood for, but their beliefs and traditions as well.

What were they to do? Their dilemma was as great as mine. What would be their response as the weeks passed by? Would it be possible for them to continue to accept us as their parsonage family under such unusual circumstances? It hardly seemed possible. Cards and letters began to arrive from individuals and groups within the congregation, expressing concern and pledging prayers. One letter in particular urged me to "press on," and closed with "keep in mind that when the going gets tough, the tough, through the grace of God, get going."

Such letters boosted my sagging morale. But others were writing letters too--not to me, but to my superior. Anonymous letters indicating that an undercurrent of suspicion and distrust was developing. One letter, a copy of which my superior chose to present to me, begged for a new minister and referred to Shirley as a "mental problem." It accused me of laxity in ministry and of "gallivanting" with Adventists, describing the congregation as "dissatisfied, grumbling, and bitter." The writer insisted the congregation was the laughingstock of the whole county, and accused me of injecting Adventism into my sermons. Referring to the congregation as "badly bruised" and the members as "outcasts" to other churches because of my wife and me, the writer asked: "Are we supposed to put up with them forever?" Furthermore, the letter accused Shirley of neglecting her family, of abandoning us, and closed with the plea: "Give us a new minister, and let Pastor Holmes find other employment." As I was trying hard to do my best under difficult circumstances, that letter was very hard to take.

While none of the accusations were true, such letters did indicate considerable antagonism. Developments over the next few months further revealed increasing opposition. Faced with an undesirable situation, and with Shirley out of the picture in another church, some members saw only one solution. They must somehow persuade me to leave. If that involved the total loss of ministry for me, that was the price they would expect me to pay.

It was not difficult to understand their feelings, for I had struggled with the temptation to adopt a equally drastic solution toward my wife. While I was delivered from that temptation, the situation is much different when many people are involved. I have no doubt that those members who campaigned for our departure wrestled with their conscience.

To be sure, I was not guiltless in the situation. With the pressures on me from home and church, my demeanor and composure were not always what they should be. Words were spoken that should never have been uttered. Needing total support and not finding it, I often felt like a caged and bewildered animal and behaved that way.

The monthly meetings of the Church Board became increasingly difficult. Each month I anticipated a new accusation of some kind, a new tale that had found its way to their ears and prejudiced attitudes.

CRITICAL MONTHS

November and December, 1969, and January, 1970, were critical. Realizing that my ministry at Sharon Lutheran Church was rapidly nearing its end, I applied for a call to another parish. None was forthcoming, church authorities saying that in view of the circumstances existing in my home, I should not expect any. That was hard to accept, especially since the Lutheran Church In America had, at least publicly, such an open ecumenical mind.

Sharing the situation with Shirley's younger brother, who was also my close and trusted friend, I discovered that he, too, realized that my ministry at Sharon would soon come to an end. Sometimes the best thing a pastor can do for his people is leave.

It is easy, in retrospect, to say that I need not have considered leaving. I believe there was enough support to stay had I pressed the matter. But that would have resulted in the alienation of some lifelong members of the congregation, whose love for their Church was deep, and who then might have felt compelled to join another Lutheran congregation. While it would have made things easier for me, it would have left bitter wounds, difficult to heal. I could not allow that to happen. What was I to do? Where was I to go? I had received no indication from the Lord that He considered me no longer fit for the ministry. The conviction that He had called me to ministry was never more certain.

The decision not to allow my problem to fracture the congregation also involved other factors. Resolving the dilemma of an ultimatum to Shirley, as well as overcoming hatred for the Bigford's, made possible a more clearheaded approach to the situation. I began to earnestly ask God to reveal His will. I was helped by a tract someone had given to me, entitled *This Thing Is From Me.*

My own prejudice and lack of knowledge about Adventism came to my attention. I had done a terrible injustice to Shirley by my previous attitude. Rather than support her, like I needed support, I condemned her like I was being condemned and was ready to believe the wildest things. Failing Shirley during her spiritual crisis, I had turned on her instead, forcing her to draw even closer to her friends for consolation and encouragement. Others turned on her too. One of my ministerial colleagues angrily said I had no business in the ministry because I couldn't keep my wife under control. None of my Lutheran ministerial colleagues, or their wives, made any attempt to call on her and minister to her or to me. How hard it is to exercise Christian love when it is needed the most!

I needed to know the truth about Adventism so that I could deal with facts not hearsay. Furthermore, if Shirley was going to be a Seventh-day Adventist, I wanted to know what she believed, and why, so that I would not speak out of ignorance. The wrong information naturally leads to the wrong conclusions. While still refusing to listen to her, I decided to read Adventist theology, in order to be accurately informed. I believed that I owed such an investigation to my family and to my congregation.

I arrived at the decision to make an honest evaluation of Seventh-day Adventism by asking and answering four questions:

1. Do you believe the Bible is the Word of God? Yes!

2. Is it your desire to conform your life to the teachings of the Word of God? Yes!

3. Do you know and understand everything in the Bible? No!

4. Should you be shown truth from the Word of God you had not known before, would you conform your life to that truth? After some hesitation, Yes!

First I read *Doctrinal Discussions,* a collection of articles by prominent Adventist theologians and pastors. The very first chapter astounded me! It dealt with the relationship of law and gospel and was so "Lutheran" that I found it difficult to believe. After the third reading I concluded that the author's understanding of the subject clearly paralleled Luther's.

Another book, entitled *Seventh-day Adventists Answer Questions on Doctrine,* intrigued me further. While also raising questions, it did cause me to realize how much I had taken for granted without investigation, such as Sunday worship, the supposed antithesis between the Old and New Testaments and between law and gospel. Furthermore, I had never considered the whole matter of the present ministry of the ascended Savior and its possible relationship with His second coming. What exactly is Jesus doing in heaven and why?

Slowly the evidence forced me to conclude that Adventism represented an honest, carefully thought through, and clearly defined understanding of the Christian faith. The many books I read were those of careful and sophisticated thinkers who presented their arguments logically and with conviction. Most impressive to me was the care and reverence with which the writers appealed to the Bible. I was not yet convinced of what they wrote, only that they wrote well and did not impress me as incompetent.

Obviously, I could not reveal my study to my congregation as it would have caused great turmoil. I took extreme care so that nothing of what I read formed the basis for my preaching. My sermons continued to be of the same tenor and content as always. I have saved them all and a simple perusal of the notes for that period supports what I have just said. Regretting the gleeful burning of Shirley's books, I wrote to Robert H. Pierson, president of the General Conference of Seventh-day Adventists, requesting more publications. In November I made a "secret" trip to Rhinelander, Wisconsin to meet the president of the Wisconsin Conference of Seventh-day Adventists, for a two hour discussion of Adventist doctrine. That trip was instrumental in arranging a subsequent visit to Andrews University in Berrien Springs, Michigan, December 3-5, 1969.

At Andrews I had interviews with three of the professors and my initial impressions were positive. However, I determined to proceed slowly and cautiously. The stakes were high, and I held a very responsible position as a spiritual leader.

After that visit to Andrews, I experienced a strange ambivalence. It seemed as though the Lord was indicating further theological study, yet I was reluctant. However, I wanted more than anything else to follow His will.

JANUARY 1970

The Church Board meeting of January 5, 1970, helped me to seriously consider study at Andrews University. Forewarned about the meeting, I prepared for it with apprehension. Anticipating what would take place, and suspecting what it might mean for my future, I spoke aloud in the quiet of my study: "Please God, don't ask me to do this; I don't want to. But if it is You, if it is really You, then I will. But You must show me clearly what You want me to do." When the meeting began I was prepared to announce my departure within six months.

Word of the meeting had gotten around the membership, and four of them had come in addition to the board members. Our friendship, especially mine, with Dr. and Mrs. Bigford was questioned. Also Shirley's membership in the Seventh-day Adventist Church. Also mentioned were ways in which they felt I was being lax in my responsibilities. It was a most disagreeable meeting for them and for me.

I polled the board on the question of my resignation. The majority asked me to stay, as did the four other members present, which surprised and delighted me. The tone of the meeting made it difficult for me to announce my resignation. But I knew that the next six months would be critical, and that I would probably have to do something about it by the end of the summer.

Subsequent events that same evening opened wide a door of possibility. Following the meeting I drove to the Bigford's to pick up my family who had been visiting that evening. While there I shared some of what had transpired at the board meeting, as well as my feelings of uncertainty about the future. After a moment of silence Dr. Bigford told me that he and *Bert*, in acknowledgement of considerable responsibility, had discussed the situation and were prepared to make an offer of assistance. Should I be interested in attending the Seventh-day Adventist Theological Seminary at Andrews University, they would support us to the amount of five hundred dollars per month for one year, with no strings attached. I would be under no obligation to join the Seventh-day Adventist Church. They would take the financial risk if I would take the theological risk. It was an exceedingly kind and generous offer under the circumstances.

That open-ended offer made it possible for me to freely consider the possibility that attendance at Andrews University might, after all, be God's will. However, I was not yet certain. Future incidents would also play their part in helping me close my ministry in Bessemer, and ultimately in the Lutheran Church.

7

BENEDICTION

Humanly speaking, my desire was to remain at Sharon Lutheran Church. I hoped the contentment and satisfaction I enjoyed there would continue for many more years.

GOD'S OTHER PLANS

God, however, had other plans for me. The growing conviction that He was in fact leading in the direction of attending Andrews University, caused me to make plans for a second visit to the campus in June. Meanwhile an event took place during the May convention of the Wisconsin-Upper Michigan Synod of the Lutheran Church In America that had a great deal to do with my decision to leave Bessemer.

An official from the headquarters of the Church was present at the meeting in an advisory capacity, and I asked for his counsel. We talked at length about Shirley's membership in the Seventh-day Adventist Church, the difficult position I was in, as well as the attitude of my congregation and the church-at-large. He informed me that it would be virtually impossible for me to obtain a call to another parish. But when he heard of the opportunity to attend Andrews, he encouraged me to do so and suggested that I make the second visit as planned. With a shrug of his arms he said: "Today ministers are crossing denominational lines all the time."

His attitude surprised me, because others had such negative attitudes toward the Adventist Church. It also disturbed me in that I anticipated greater support from my Church. I expected him to assure me that I need have no fear about present or future service, and that I would have the complete support of the denomination. Instead, in the kindest way possible, he gently indicated that my evangelistic approach to ministry, and my conservative theology, were not fully appreciated in any case. I asked if he would send me his counsel in writing, and he did so.

While my disappointment was acute, the incident helped greatly in the development of the conviction that God indeed had something new in store.

SUMMER VISIT TO ANDREWS

Arriving back in Bessemer, I lost no time in writing to Andrews University, asking if they would allow me to visit during the summer term and attend some classes as an observer. The dean of the seminary, Dr. W. G. C. Murdoch, responded warmly and assured me of a welcome.

The first week of my summer vacation was spent in Waukegan, Illinois where I helped reroof the home of my mother's only sister. Three days completed the job, but while working in the hot sun, away from home and parish, I had second thoughts. Deciding not to visit Andrews, I traveled instead to Chicago to visit a trusted friend, who was a Lutheran theologian.

We spent most of Saturday together and shared our thoughts on theology, the ministry, and the condition and trends of the Church. In view of the fact that I changed my mind about visiting Andrews University, I did not even mention it to him.

In the course of our conversation he looked at me and said: "Ray, this is an apostate Church." His remark astounded me, for he was a thorough and careful thinker, not prone to make rash statements.

"Why do you say that?" I inquired.

"Because this Church does not rely on the Holy Spirit, but on programs," he answered.

At any other time his words would not have caused such turmoil in my mind. Since my concerns about liberal theological and ecumenical trends had a long history, the same thought had entered my mind more than once. His verbalizing of the thought, in the context of the particular circumstances, made our conversation highly significant.

We retired for the night, but I could not sleep. Ordinarily I would fall asleep within sixty seconds, but not that night. I tossed and turned. My mind churning with my

54

friend's words. Finally I said aloud to the Lord: "All right. If You let me sleep, I will go to Andrews tomorrow as planned." Instantly I fell asleep.

In the morning, Sunday, we attended worship together and then had dinner. Afterward I told him where I was going. As I departed he put his hand on my shoulder, and said: "Ray, when the time comes you will know what to do." How thankful I was, and am, for such a wise and understanding Christian friend!

Arriving at Andrews University later that day, I checked in at the Campus Center where the seminary had reserved a room for me. The next morning I planned to visit several classes. Before leaving my room I prayed and asked the Lord to lead me to some students, because I needed more than information. I needed impressions. At that stage impressions were most important. I wanted to talk with as many seminary students as possible in order to ascertain whether or not they experienced personal relationships with Christ. The first class I attended dealt with the interpretation of the book of Revelation from the original Greek language. It proved very interesting, and the contents of the lecture were intriguing.

At the close of the two-hour session the students filed out of the classroom one by one. I watched them go until the room emptied. The last man out suddenly wheeled about in the doorway and, making his way through the seats, came toward me with his hand outstretched. "I'm Bob Leake," he said. "What's your name?"

I gave him my name and informed him that I was a Lutheran pastor engaged in *spying out* the seminary. We laughed together, then sat and talked. Learning that I would be on campus all day, he graciously invited me to supper, where I met his children and his charming wife Jean.

The Lord certainly answered my morning prayer. With captivating humor and charm the Leake's made me feel right at home as they shared their experience of becoming Seventh-day Adventists. That evening in their home, I ate my first vegetarian meal.

At my request a number of students were invited over. Following supper, we spent several meaningful hours in sharing our relationship with Christ. I played a tape of one of my recent sermons because I wanted to hear their reactions. They seemed to enjoy it, and one of them remarked: "Sounds like a good Adventist message." I knew then that they appreciated the expository preaching of the evangelical gospel. We did have something in common! I questioned them at length concerning their faith, and by their testimonies I knew they all had vital relationships with Jesus Christ.

The next day I attended more classes and visited with the professors I met during my previous visit in December. With the impressive impressions of the personal faith life of Adventist seminary students and professors on my mind, I traveled that night to my sister's home in Illinois. There I spent a day and a half in deep thought. I searched and searched for the loophole in the circumstances that would permit me to avoid what appeared to be God's will. But there was none.

The next evening, weary of mental wrestling, I curled up on the couch and buried myself in a history book. My sister's family was watching the telecast of a Billy Graham crusade. Paying no attention, I remained absorbed in my book. Then Dr. Graham read his preaching text and I sat up to give it my full attention:

> *Therefore, since we are surrounded by so great a cloud of witnesses, let us also lay aside every weight, and sin which clings so closely, and let us run with perseverance the race that is set before us, looking to Jesus the pioneer and perfecter of our faith, who for the joy that was set before him endured the cross, despising the shame, and is seated at the right hand of the throne of God. (Hebrews 12:1-2)*

Dr. Graham went on to compare the Christian life to a football game, which must be played according to the rules. He illustrated that the Ten Commandments represented Christian life-style. It was as though God was reaffirming many of the thoughts bombarding my brain cells.

Once again unable to fall asleep immediately, I cast about for one good reason to avoid making a decision. I found none. I also could not sleep. Finally, again, I told the Lord: "If you let me sleep, I'll decide in the morning." Instantly I fell into a deep and satisfying sleep.

Waking early, I spent two hours mentally reliving every single event of the previous two years, every circumstance, every step, every conversation, searching for a way to avoid what I was certain then to be God's desire. Finally I said to Him aloud:

All right, Lord, if You want me to go to Andrews University, I will do so. When I get home I will begin to take the necessary steps. If I am making a mistake, misreading what seems to be Your will, You must be responsible for stopping me.

Later my sister took one look at me and said: "You've made a decision haven't you?"

"Yes, I have," I answered. "How did you know?"

"I could see it on your face. You look relaxed and at peace."

And I was!

Upon returning to Bessemer, I applied to Andrews as a graduate student and reserved an apartment for September.

RESIGNATION

On July 18, 1970, I addressed a letter of resignation to the congregation and read it publicly, as was customary, the next Sunday.

It is with gratitude to God and to the members of Sharon that I look back upon the seven years of ministry here. However, believing that God is calling me to a new phase of Christian experience, a leave-taking has become necessary. . . My prayers shall always be with the members of Sharon, that God will lead and guide into all the truth and sustain and strengthen the believers for the age in which we have been called to live and bear witness to salvation in Jesus Christ. I trust you all to God.

Following the worship services that Sunday, my family and I left for the remainder of my summer vacation, which lasted three weeks. When I returned there were five Sundays of preaching ministry before our departure for Andrews University. What should I say to my people? How could I best serve them? As I pondered and prayed, I realized that the last five sermons should help the congregation to understand what was happening in my life, and to prepare them for possible future events in my life and theirs.

57

LAST SERMONS

For the first message I chose Philippians 1:27 to 2:16 as my text. I said:

Let me ask you, Do you think that what has happened in my life and that of my wife has no meaning or relevance for you? You would make a grave mistake if you believe that you can discount the events of the past year. God has been speaking to you through these events. He continues to do so. And He will do so long after we are gone from your midst. Quench not the Holy Spirit! These are matters of life and death! Eternity hinges on the response we make when God speaks to us.

The theme for the second sermon came from Ephesians 5:15-21. That Sunday I told my church members:

I have no desire to leave you with flowery words and empty phrases, but with admonitions and challenges for the future. I believe God is giving the members of this church a gracious opportunity to come to grips with truth. God wants to bring a spiritual revival to this church and to begin it in YOUR heart. There is no meaning to, or reason for, life without the truth of God's Word. Some of it is hard truth, but that is necessary because we have such hard hearts.

The text for the third sermon was Ephesians 3:7-21. During the third sermon I said:

Paul had feeling for his people. He knew the believers were disturbed and upset by his experiences. His words were designed to reassure them and help them find meaning in what he was going through. He was in jail! Can you imagine the questions his flock was asking? Why has this happened to our pastor? Why has God allowed this development in his life? They would be confused and uncertain, feel threatened and insecure. But Paul counsels them not to lose heart, turning their thoughts to God's wisdom and will. Paul was a persistent fisherman. He always fished in the waters where God placed him. Wherever the Lord in His wisdom sees fit to send me, and wherever there are ears eager to hear and minds to understand, I shall by His grace preach Christ!

For the fourth message I took 2 Timothy 4:1-8 as my text, and among other things, said:

I believe we are in the time prophesied by Paul when theologians, church leaders, publishing houses, members of churches, are not so interested in hearing the plain, unvarnished truth of the Word of God, which is able to make us wise for salvation. Not so interested in what the Bible actually says, but prefer to follow their own ideas or tradition. Theology is in a shambles today. This has filtered down from the seminaries over the past decade, and now is reaching the people in the pews and the children in the classrooms. This is so relevant for you as a congregation, as you are now faced with the necessity of calling a new pastor. I make bold to say that this congregation will get the kind of pastor it wants. If you want a man who is theologically liberal, who does not believe in evangelism and conversion, then you will get him. What do you want? Rather, what do you think God wants for His church?

Acts 20:18-32, 36-38 from the *Living Bible* was the text for my final sermon to Sharon Lutheran Church. As things turned out it was also the last sermon I would preach to a Lutheran congregation. It would be my final word of counsel and encouragement to people I had served and loved in the Lord for seven happy and eventful years. Paul's last message to his congregation at Ephesus consisted of three reminders. 1-He reminds them of his ministry and message, 2-He reminds them of their responsibility and assignment, and 3-He reminds them of their source of faith and strength. Then I concluded by saying:

When he had finished speaking, he knelt and prayed with them, and they wept aloud as they embraced him in farewell, sorrowing most of all because he said that he would never see them again. Then they accompanied him down to the ship. It was a good parting. He had admonished them and counseled them in a final message.

They had listened, and we can assume with the determination to heed his words. They said farewell and took him to the ship. He set his eyes toward Jerusalem, where work awaited him, where there were other people who needed to hear of the "necessity of turning from sin to God through faith in our Lord Jesus Christ." And the elders? What did they do? After the tears, the good-byes, and the waves from the shore, they turned and walked back to their village, their congregation, their assignment, their place--with the same message![1]

At the close of the worship service I pronounced the benediction upon my people:

The Lord bless you and keep you, the Lord make His face to shine upon you, and be gracious to you. The Lord lift up His countenance upon you and give you peace. In the name of the Father, and of the Son, and of the Holy Spirit.

In response they all sang the "Amen."

One by one I shook their hands as my ministry as their pastor came to its end. I could not speak, only nod and occasionally whisper a soft "Thank you!"

When the last one left I turned to face the empty sanctuary where I had preached, celebrated Holy Communion, baptized, married, buried, for seven years of my life. Most congregations do not stop to think that the years a pastor spends with them is a gift of time out of his life, which can never be recovered. I went to my study, removed my clerical vestments, and carefully folded them away.

Returning to the familiar vaulted sanctuary I paused for one last moment beside the pulpit, touched it with my hand and offered a prayer of thanksgiving for my ministry there. Then, with a final "Amen," which echoed off ceiling and walls, I walked out and away.

---

[1] Those five sermons were recorded and are available on cassette through POINTER Publications.

8

DIGGING DEEPER

We left Bessemer in a borrowed car, as our little Volkswagen was not powerful enough to pull our belongings in the rented U-Haul trailer. We moved into a student apartment at Andrews University and prepared for academic life once again.

UNIQUE SITUATION

The students and faculty warmly received us. Word had preceded us that a Lutheran minister, whose wife had become a Seventh-day Adventist, was coming to study at the seminary. Friends informed me later that while pastors of other denominations had taken some courses from the seminary and university, it was the first time such an individual had come with the express purpose of making an investigation of exactly what the Seventh-day Adventist Church believes and preaches. It turned out to be a unique situation both for me and the seminary.

Still seeking impressions as well as information, I was most interested in the life of the seminary and eagerly began to make friends. I wanted to talk as much as possible with teachers and students alike, both in and out of the class-room. Many of the students were curious, too, and did not hesitate to ask me questions about my ministry and Lutheran theology. Speaking with the professors, I learned of their readiness to give of their time in answering any questions I might have. Each one invited me to raise questions and challenge their thought at any time. It was an exceedingly generous offer. During each ten week quarter, the instructors must cover a certain amount of material and, therefore, needed every moment. Thankful for the openness with which they received me, I took advantage of the opportunity to ask questions and make comments. Mostly, however, I preferred to listen, to read, to think, and to weigh the evidence presented.

I arrived at the seminary with a chip on my shoulder and with the hope of discovering heresies so that I could explain them to Shirley and win her back to Lutheranism. While believing it to be God's will that I attend Andrews University, I did not yet believe it His will to leave the Lutheran ministry. Perhaps, I reasoned, God had given me the opportunity not only to win back my wife but also to help others who might be tempted to believe the doctrines of Adventism. Perhaps I could even help the Bigfords to find their way out of legalism to a faith relationship with Christ based solely on His grace.

It was apparent to all concerned that I was extremely sensitive about my position. By the grace of God I was able to face each day and each class lecture with some degree of composure. As the only non-Adventist enrolled in the seminary I felt very much alone, isolated, surrounded, hemmed in on all sides by an unusual and difficult experience. How grateful I was--and am--for their patience and understanding. It was difficult for the professors too, to have a stranger in their classes weighing, and critical of, every statement and theological assertion.

Hedwig Jemison, who at the time was secretary to the seminary Dean, has told me repeatedly how conscious everyone was that they were "walking on eggs" in our daily relationships. However, their genuine concern and love for me, without in one instance compromising their beliefs, were apparent and served to inhibit my tongue when I was tempted to make rash and unkind remarks. There were moments when that temptation was very strong indeed. Especially as I began to realize that there might just be a great deal of truth to the doctrines unique to Adventism. As I listened, read, and thought, I realized more and more that the kind of Adventist theology I was hearing was a well-thought-through, logical, and conservative interpretation of the Word of God. To my growing amazement and delight, I discovered that while Adventists revere and utilize the writings of Ellen G. White in formulating their theology, the Bible is the primary source. Adventist doctrine is based upon, and proven, from the Word of God, not Mrs. White as many critics charge. Her writings are viewed as inspired commentary on the teachings of the Bible.

INNER BATTLE

As the days and weeks passed, the battle within me grew fierce. I came to discover the truth and set myself to the task, come what may. But, like most people, when faced with the truth I resisted it. As I dug deeper into Adventist beliefs, I feared the excavation would collapse upon me and bury me in Adventism. I didn't want to leave the Lutheran Church. "Kicking and screaming," I resisted Adventist theology. Yet, at the same time, an irresistible desire to find out as much as possible drove me relentlessly on.

Still adamantly refusing to listen to Shirley's testimony, even after almost two years, I left our apartment each day for the books and classes that would ultimately, and so drastically, change my life once again. What the Adventist students read once, I read several times, checking and rechecking with Scripture. At times it grew wearisome, and I would slam a book shut in exasperation and irritation. Frequently I cocked my eyes heavenward to chide God, suggesting He didn't know what He was doing. One day, while trudging to class through a blustery Michigan winter storm, I yelled into the wind: "You've really goofed this time, Lord!" The moment uttered, my words were snatched away by the bitterly cold wind. Gone. As though they had never been spoken.

Shirley could only watch me struggle, and pray for me. Being at Andrews University obviously answered part of her prayers for me, the rest she could only leave to the Holy Spirit. We were still strangers to each other spiritually speaking, so close yet so far.

The crisis occurred about the middle of the first quarter. Things were not turning out the way I anticipated. I was still there. Still studying. No radical heresies sent me fleeing from the campus in horror. On the contrary, I was intrigued by the faculty's Biblical approach and began to see the truth in Adventist theology. Yet, at the same time, I was rebelling against it, refusing to accept it.

The critical hour is still vivid in my mind. One of the courses I took was the Doctrine of the Atonement. During the first five weeks the professor carefully laid the Biblical basis for the Adventist view of that vital Christian doctrine.

Revealing the relationship between the sacrificial death of Christ on the cross and the Old Testament Tabernacle ritual of atonement, he then began to consider Christ's role as High Priest in the heavenly sanctuary as portrayed in the book of Hebrews, as well as its connection with the atonement. Protestants have generally believed that Christ's death on the cross completed the atonement. Adventist theology considers that Christ made atonement for sin on Calvary and that He ministers the benefits of that atoning death to the world and to God's people in His role as High Priest. Furthermore, atonement involves not only the *assurance* of victory over the power of Satan but also the *actuality* of final victory when Satan is destroyed and God's character stands vindicated before the entire universe.

Beginning to see new and profound significance in the cross of Christ in relation to His post-resurrection ministry in heaven, the buildup of inner tension was explosive. Three years in a Lutheran seminary, and ten years of interpreting the Bible and preaching, had done their job. To have my thoughts and perceptions stretched out of comfortable patterns proved distressing. The tension increased until one morning I almost bolted from classroom 230. I forced myself to sit it out as I sensed that a significant moment had arrived. Confronting the lecturer after class, I asked him if I could talk with him a moment. Sensing my agitation, he indicated his next hour was free and invited me to his office. It was very difficult to verbally express what was happening inside of me.

I started to explain that I was undergoing an identity crisis--a Lutheran yet not a Lutheran as opposed to not an Adventist yet an Adventist--but my words ended in a flood of tears. Haltingly, between sobs, I tried to express how I felt, how difficult everything had become, what a dilemma I faced. Tears have always come hard for me. I can count on one hand the number of times I've cried in adult life, but that morning my intense need wrenched the tears forth.

Then I heard someone else sobbing and turned to see my teacher--who that morning became my friend--joining me in the fellowship of distress. He wasn't crying *for* me, He cried *with* me. I accepted his gift of tears because I needed it, and because it helped. We cried together. We talked together. Then we prayed together.

That morning I could have fled the campus, but I had no automobile. Just before leaving Bessemer I had purchased a Volkswagen squareback, a vehicle too light to pull a fully loaded trailer. To get the trailer to Berrien Springs, we borrowed a car from the Bigfords. Shortly after a visit from Mrs. Bigford, when we exchanged cars, Shirley was involved in a three car collision. Hit from behind while stopped for a turn, the badly damaged VW spent almost two months in repair. Without transportation it would have been difficult to leave the campus. I could not even travel to my sister's home to share my struggle with her. I had to face it alone. But God redeemed those circumstances also in that they served to keep me isolated at Andrews during a critical time. While I had the temptation to run, I had no way of doing so.

Leaving the office of my teacher/friend, I went to our apartment and there prayed some more. Telling the Lord that I didn't understand what was happening or why, I begged Him for some assurance that I should continue. Opening my Bible, I chanced to read in Habbakuk until I came to chapter 1, verse 5, "Look among the nations, and see; wonder and be astounded. For I am doing a work in your days that you would not believe if told."

A feeling of assurance came over me. I knew then that I must continue to "look," to "wonder and be astounded." I knew also that the time had not yet come for me to understand why, for I would not believe it anyway. But I did receive from the passage the assurance that one day I would know, understand, and appreciate God's guidance.

COMPATIBILITY

The entire experience of over two years caused me to do a lot of thinking about faith. What is faith? In essence it is *trust* in the person of Jesus Christ no matter how or where He leads. The route may seem strange and confusing, but it will lead to blessing and greater trust in the wisdom of God. If we seek to be obedient to the Lord, we cannot shut our minds to further knowledge and growth. We need not fear truth, but welcome it. The Psalmist pleads, "Oh send out thy light and thy truth; let them lead me, let them bring me to thy holy hill and to thy dwelling!" (Psalm 43:3) Also, "Behold, thou desirest truth in the inward being; therefore teach me wisdom in my secret heart." (Psalm 51:6) If more truth exists, the believer must desire it, learn it, welcome it, accept it, apply it, live by it, and teach it to others. I was learning that Adventism was not something to fear and reject, but that it might be something to love and embrace.

I was learning to love Adventists too. Love grows with understanding. Those we often see as unlovable and unlovely suddenly become objects of love when understood. I discovered that, by and large, Adventists are fine people with high standards of faith, morality, ethics, and human concern. To be sure, they are not perfect--none of us are--but they desire to love God and worship Him, and to love and serve their fellowman. The fact that most Adventist Christians spend two and a half hours in church every Sabbath morning in study and worship reveals some of their love for God and man. They also express it by the fact that Adventists are some of the most sacrificial givers and support one of the widest and most farflung mission endeavors. Their willingness to sacrifice and their mission outreach overwhelmed me.

Amazed at the monthly reports of large-scale baptisms in mission fields where many mainline denominations are phasing out, I wanted to discover why Seventh-day Adventism is having such success. One answer is in the fervent hope and anticipation among Adventists of Christ's imminent return. Contrary to what many think, this belief has not resulted in a dreary otherworldliness. It serves, rather, to awaken a deep concern for the salvation of individuals and a willingness to help them by means of social welfare and medical assistance. Thus, while eagerly facing the future, Seventh-day Adventists live in the midst of present-day reality.

I could identify with this emphasis, for I had preached the return of Christ for ten years. I recall in my first parish how a number of people gratefully thanked me for my sermons on Christ's second advent, a message they had not heard for some time. Looking through my old sermon notes, I discovered to my amazement how many of them concerned the second advent or alluded to it. Having arrived at the conclusion, from Bible study and from knowledge of world and church conditions, that Christ's return is imminent, I had no difficulty accepting the Seventh-day Adventist teaching on His return.

As I studied further, I discovered a common ground with the Adventist Church's understanding of creation: we both believe that God formed the earth in six literal days of twenty-four hours. Many conservative Lutherans still believe in a literal six-day creation. Adventism, however, opened up a new dimension to creationism with its doctrine of the restoration of the creation to its pristine perfection in the new heaven and the new earth after Christ's return. God, who made the earth, will utterly and completely destroy Satan, the wicked, and all the residue of evil. Then He will purge the earth with fire and re-create it in its original condition. His people will dwell in Edenic perfection for all eternity. (See Malachi 4:1-3; Isaiah 65:17; Revelation 21:3-4.)

For a long time I realized that the entire Bible rests upon the historicity and accuracy of the book of Genesis. It records the creation account, the establishment of the Sabbath, the headship principle that is foundational to family and congregational life, and the rebellion of mankind. Without the actuality of Adam's sin of disobedience as described in Genesis, the sacrifice of Christ has no meaning.

Holding such views became more difficult as time went by as they no longer represented the prevailing opinion of my denomination. In the SDA Theological Seminary at Andrews University I found a body of people who believed firmly as I did about the relationship of Christ to the Bible. Once again I realized even more strongly that today the Christian needs more than faith in a nebulous Christ. The Christian needs informed faith--Biblically informed faith--in order to face the falsehood and apostasy which parodies true Christianity.

In addition, I found compatibility with Adventists on the wholeness of man. For a long time I believed God was interested in the whole person--body , soul, and mind. In Adventism I saw such a belief put into practice. Christian faith is not a philosophy, but an entire way of life. The grace of God offers the gift of the good news concerning salvation, and the good life lived in fellowship with Him and according to the principles for the good life. If an individual is concerned with having an obedient relationship with Christ, he will take care of his body also. He will abstain from all harmful substances such as tobacco, alcohol, and drugs. The Christian will take care of his body as a response of faith in Christ who has redeemed him. Paul wrote:

> *May the God of peace himself make you entirely pure and devoted to God; and may your spirit and soul and body be kept strong and blameless until that day when*

our Lord Jesus Christ comes back again. (1 Thess. 5:23, *Living Bible.*)

Believing that sanctification of the body is also a part of God's will, and that God desires to move the Christian in the direction of perfection, the believer will voluntarily--with the aid of the Holy Spirit--abstain from everything harmful to the body. God's Word says: "I am praying that all is well with you and that your body is as healthy as I know your soul is." (3 John 2, *Living Bible.*) It involves taking seriously God's care for the whole person.

Because He has made us with a free will, He does not coerce; rather, He informs. He presents us with truth and divine guidance through revelation. Then He lets us make a choice. If we decide to follow His plan for us, He empowers us to do so by the Holy Spirit. Having believed and preached for many years that God was calling His people in our age to a radically distinctive life-style indicating their relationship to God, it was with growing excitement that I realized the Seventh-day Adventist Church called for exactly that. As I found more and more common ground between Adventism and my beliefs, I began to feel less of a stranger at Andrews, less out of place, more able to view Shirley with understanding. She had made her decision, I realized, not on the basis of a friendship but on truth. I, as well as many others, had grossly misjudged her and scandalously condemned her. The barrier between us began to erode away. She became less and less the stranger in my home.

CATCHING THE VISION

Slowly, as the weeks went by, I began to catch a vision of the mission of the Seventh-day Adventist Church. It did represent the distinctive life-style I felt today's world needed. The various emphases of its total message to mankind contains the resources for meeting all the pressing spiritual-physical-mental needs of contemporary people. Its major emphases are:

1. Emphasis on the Bible as the Word of God in a day when trust in the Bible as God's Word has been undermined and its inspiration denied.
2. Emphasis on personal salvation in a day when a major concern of many churches is meeting social needs.

3. Emphasis on God's Law (particularly the Ten Commandments) in a day of lawlessness, licentiousness, and widespread disregard of God's plan for life both within and without the Church.

4. Emphasis on prophecy in a day when most people believe God has never spoken and that the future is a ghastly prospect.

5. Emphasis on Christ's High Priestly ministry of daily care in a day when most people feel nobody really cares.

6. Emphasis on health in a day of dissipation and little personal, disciplined care for the human body.

7. Emphasis on a distinctive Sabbath in a day when materialism has eroded most sacred observances.

8. Emphasis on the second Advent of Christ in a day when man has adopted either extreme humanistic optimism in the belief that he will solve all his pressing problems, or extreme pessimism fearing no hope exists at all.

As I dug deeper into Adventist theology, I was exposed to more and more principles of truth. Although thoroughly Biblical, centuries of tradition had buried many of them. Luther and other Reformers of the sixteenth century had unearthed some. With respect to others, it remained for the nineteenth-to-twentieth-century reformation to call them to the attention of the world and of the Christian Church at-large.

That God created the Seventh-day Adventist Church to be the instrument He would use to spearhead today's religious reformation became a conviction during December, 1970, and in the early months of 1971. Decision time was coming again.

9

GOD MADE MY DECISION

At first glance the title of this chapter may give the reader the impression that I am trying to escape responsibility for my actions and blame them on God. It is not my intention to excuse and rationalize my decision to join the Seventh-day Adventist Church. But that God was leading I have no doubt whatsoever.

CAPTIVATING NATURE OF TRUTH

I do want to make the point that God's truth can so capture a person, that it takes charge of one's life. When the Christian comes face to face with truth he has a choice to make. The nature of his surrender to the lordship of Christ will determine how he chooses. The Christian's greatest desire is to be in an obedient relationship with the Lord.

Of course I am referring to positive and not negative truth--truth that blesses and brings good as opposed to bad. It is certainly true that the use of drugs, alcohol, and tobacco, harms the human body. Because the consequences of such truth are negative and harmful one must refrain. Truth can protect as well as inform. To learn truth which warns is a blessing. On the other hand, to discover truth which enlarges and enhances one's understanding and appreciation of God's love and revelation is an even greater blessing. Such truth builds up rather than tears down, encourages rather than discourages, and promotes spiritual growth rather than inhibit it. Such truth should always be welcomed.

One of the most severe criticisms of the Seventh-day Adventist Church is that it seeks to persuade Christians from other churches to join it. For a time I echoed the same charge. But what does one do if he has received further insight and understanding of the Word of God? Does he keep it to himself? To answer "yes" would constitute a denial of the very nature of the Christian faith-life. Not only is the believer under divine mandate to communicate God's truth, but an inner compulsion compels him to do so. What God reveals must be communicated and shared.

Therefore, in spite of all the criticism and opposition, the Christian must share the truth. The Bible pictures the believer as light, as salt, as leaven in the world. Light, salt, and yeast affect their surroundings. Scriptural truth is God's truth. The Church is God's Church. The labels attached to various denominations do not appear in the Word of God. The Bible does not recognize Roman Catholics, Presbyterians, Baptists, Lutherans, etc. Nowhere does it mention the name *Seventh-Day Adventist.*

Instead, the Bible calls the Church the "people of God," the "body of Christ," the "fellowship of the saints," as well as a "holy temple." In those passages which speak of the closing hours of earth's history, Scripture refers to the church as the "gathered" and the "remnant." Remnant means those left over, the last. Revelation 14:12 describes that group of Christian believers as "those who keep the commandments of God and the faith of Jesus."

There is no doubt in my mind that we are now living in human history's last age, and that God's Spirit will gather a final group of followers to prepare for Christ's return. The question is: Where can they be found? Revelation 18:4 tells us that God's people appear in all denominations, but it also indicates that God is calling them out to escape His judgment upon faithlessness and apostasy.

Because the Seventh-day Adventist Church believes it has received the message and mission described in Revelation 14-18, it seeks to be obedient and faithful. It responds in deep humility. To keep Adventists humble God addressed the letter to the Laodiceans to the last church, which urges it to repent of its lukewarmness (Revelation 3:14-22). Therefore, it is not with bravado, arrogance, or a condemnatory spirit that the Adventist Church fulfills its mission, but in dependence on God's grace and power and in the realization of its own imperfection and need. It is also conscious of the fact that it, too, will be held accountable for faithfulness and adherence to God's written revelation.

According to the Bible, the remnant consists of those believers who keep the commandments of God, all of them, and who base their salvation solely on the shed blood of Christ and faith in Him, identifying marks of the Seventh-day Adventist Church.

After much study and investigation I was convinced that the Seventh-day Adventist Church does in fact represent that remnant. It seeks to do so both in its theology and in its life-style. To be sure, not all of its individual members are prime examples of either theology or life-style, yet one must not judge or condemn the whole church as a result. Once again we must allow the Word of God rather than the disappointing witness of outward adherents to serve as our guide. In the final analysis, the test as to whether Adventist or non-Adventist Christians belong to the remnant will be whether or not they are obedient to God's commandments and have faith in Christ. The questions each individual must ask are: Am I faithful to the Bible's description of the remnant people of God? Do I believe in Jesus and keep God's commandments, including the seventh-day Sabbath which is Saturday?

SABBATH OR SUNDAY?

When I asked these questions of myself, I had to answer "No." Though I believed in Jesus, I was not observing the Biblical Sabbath, Saturday, the seventh day of the week. During three years of training in a Lutheran seminary, and ten years as a Lutheran minister, I never studied the question of Sabbath versus Sunday. Sunday was taken for granted as the right worship day because most of Christianity kept Sunday and Luther wrote nothing critical of the practice.

Unquestioningly, I accepted the traditional view that the Christian church observed Sunday because Christ's resurrection took place on the first day of the week, and also because the Christian was no longer considered to be under the Law. This latter aspect we will consider in a subsequent chapter.

Part of my decision to attend Andrews University involved finding out the truth about Sunday observance and the seventh-day Sabbath. For ten years I ministered in a religious tradition which observed various yearly festivals such as Christmas, Epiphany, Easter, Pentecost, Trinity, Ash Wednesday, All Saints Day, Palm Sunday, Good Friday, the Transfiguration and many others. When one takes the Bible alone as his guide to Christian festivals, it becomes immediately clear that none of these are specifically mentioned for special celebration by the Christian church. Certainly all of the events which they symbolize are part of the New Testament narrative of Christ's life, but nowhere does Scripture instruct Christians to pay special attention to those events on particular days.

When one faces the issue squarely and does not permit ages of church tradition and contemporary culture to determine the conclusion, the clarity of the seventh-day Sabbath is startling. The Decalogue, the Ten Commandments, commands the observance of the seventh-day Sabbath. However, it did not originate there. The seventh-day Sabbath was part of creation. God set it apart for all of mankind. Therefore the argument that of all the commandments the Sabbath commandment pertains only to the Jews, does not stand up. Nowhere does the Biblical account make such a distinction, whereas tradition and/or culture does.

If we apply the Protestant principle of Bible interpretation which holds that the Bible is to be interpreted literally unless the context indicates otherwise, then more than the principle of Sabbath observance is valid. The specific day itself is also part of faithfulness to the commandment. Furthermore, the observance of the seventh-day Sabbath was not simply a part of Jewish culture anymore than the other nine. Individuals have challenged Sabbath observance by saying there is no difference between one day and the next. My answer is: "That is true, except if God has spoken and declared there is a difference." If God has spoken then that ought to be enough.

Our Lord's criticism of tradition as religious criteria appears in Matthew 15:1-9 and Mark 7:5-13. He accuses the Scribes and Pharisees of transgressing God's commandment in favor of their own tradition and, by so doing, nullifying the Word of God. Jesus quoted Isaiah 29:13 to them: "This people honors me with their lips, but their heart is far from me; in vain do they worship me, teaching as doctrines the precepts of men." (Matthew 15:8-9) Christ's words made it clear that I could not, and must not, follow tradition but the Word of God.

The hallowing of the seventh-day Sabbath immediately followed the creation of humans. God created people dependant upon Him and with the need to rest and worship. Next He provided them with the time and opportunity to do so. Furthermore, He motivated us to rest and worship by attaching the blessing of holiness to the seventh day. The Sabbath was to be the memorial of creation by which God would be perpetually acknowledged as Creator and the source of life. It would also assist people in acknowledging their dependance upon God.

Therefore, we cannot consider it legalistic to observe the seventh-day Sabbath. Rather, it is an act of faith in response to a loving Creator and Redeemer. However, we can rightly regard it as legalistic to observe a day which God did not command and hallow and which only human tradition has established. Biblical, historical, and theological evidence all indicate that God created the seventh-day Sabbath for the benefit of all people, and that He has never abrogated it.

The Gospels mention the first day of the week in only six places: Matthew 28:1; Mark 16:2, 9; Luke 24:1; John 20:1, 19. We must discover authority for Sunday as a holy day in these passages if we are to find it at all. But they say nothing about a change in the Sabbath. They give no special title to the first day of the week, but call the seventh the Sabbath. Nor do they command us to observe the first day. Instead, they simply refer to things that took place on the first day of the week as opposed to another day. The New Testament writers always carefully distinguished between the Sabbath and other week days. (Compare Luke 23:56 with 24:1.)

Ample historical evidence reveals that Sunday observance began at an early date in the tradition of the church. But it had no Biblical authority behind it. Opposition to anything Jewish encouraged the change, as well as the activity of the "mystery of lawlessness" (2 Thessalonians 2:7), forces already at work in the time of the early church. In spite of this early trend, many Christians observed the seventh-day Sabbath for hundreds of years. Never totally abandoned by Christians, the continuing seventh-day Sabbath provides one of the seeds for reformation in our own day.

The Gospels clearly indicate Christ's attitude toward the Sabbath. Consider Luke 4:16: "And he came to Nazareth, where he had been brought up; and he went to the synagogue, as his custom was, on the sabbath day." Proponents of Sunday observance, and I was one of them, explain away such passages on the grounds that His evangelistic zeal took Him to the place where, and at times when, He knew people would gather. But notice the emphasis in the verse upon His "custom." In other words, He habitually went to the Synagogue on the Sabbath because He was obedient to His Father's will. His custom involved not only His evangelistic concern, but also His own personal piety and observance of the day.

Jesus made a number of significant statements about the Sabbath, statements that did not do away with it but which would restore the Sabbath to its rightful and original place in the worship life of His people. To the Pharisees who condemned His disciples for, on the Sabbath, picking some grain to eat, He said: "The Sabbath was made for man, not man for the Sabbath!" (Mark 2:27-28) In no way can His statement be construed to mean the abrogation of the Sabbath, especially in light of Matthew 5:17-19.

First of all, in His statement Jesus asserts the universal nature of the Sabbath, it is for all people not just for the Jews. Just as He is the Saviour of the whole world and not only for the Jews. Second, He declares that the Sabbath is a blessing not a burden. While He recognized the perverted concept of the Sabbath that prevailed at that time, He was not, as some authors contend, canceling out the entire postexilic Sabbath theology. God still required Sabbath reformation and restoration. Christ was quite aware that people were not experiencing the blessings of the Sabbath because of the legalistic context it had received over the centuries. Its observance had become a hardship. But that did not mean He condoned rebellion and disregard of one of the Father's clear commands.

Jesus took the Sabbath out of the legalistic context Jewish tradition had evolved about it and put it into the context of grace when He said: "The Son of man is lord even of the sabbath." He didn't say the Sabbath no longer existed. Nor did He say that He Himself would take the place of the Sabbath in the same way that He became the Paschal Lamb. He did, however, declare that He is the Sabbath's Lord. In other words, Sabbath observance must begin with faith in Him! Therefore, no person can rightly keep the seventh day as the Biblical Sabbath until or unless he acknowledges Jesus Christ as Lord. Sabbath rest begins with rest from sin by faith in the Sin Bearer and Saviour.

True Sabbathkeeping is not legalistic works, but represents a faith/love response to the person of Jesus Christ. As for which day is truly the seventh, ask any Jew. Never once in their history have they lost track of the Sabbath.

The Sabbath has more significance than a discussion of Saturday as opposed to Sunday would seem to indicate. A memorial of creation, the Sabbath has implications for ecology as well as the relationship between races. If God's Sabbath had been kept down through history, and stewardship over the creation taken seriously, the world ecological mess would be considerably reduced. Because humans have consistently refused to accept and acknowledge their creatureliness, their role as created beings, the earth has been methodically exploited and destroyed. God made us to have dominion over the earth and subdue it, but we have perverted this responsibility and exploited the earth, ruining it instead.

As a memorial of creation the Sabbath tells all human beings of their common origin, no matter what their color. It declares to all races that God is their Father and, consequently, they are brothers. The Sabbath is a reminder that no matter how meticulously we prepare for its observance, if we harbor any hatred or prejudice toward any member of the human family, our preparation is incomplete. Furthermore, hatred and prejudice effectively cancel out our Sabbathkeeping and render our worship void and meaningless. Jesus said: "I desire mercy, and not sacrifice." (Matthew 9:13)

The proclamation of the Sabbath should greatly comfort modern people in their terror of the swift passage of time. Having too often rejected the past, and viewing the future with fear, they see the passing of time as bringing them closer to the abyss of nothingness. Time appears as an unrelenting enemy. Yet it really is a friend.

God considers time significant and has set aside a specific period of twenty-four hours each week to indicate that fact. The Sabbath can remind us of Christ's return because it represents a divine interruption of the week that previews the great intervention of the second advent. For me, the Sabbath proclaims that time's swift passage brings us closer and closer to eternal fellowship with Christ in the New Jerusalem.

How, I have been asked, is it possible for God to make a period of time holy? After all, time cannot be seen or touched or smelled. The answer, of course, is the same way in which He declares anything to be holy, such as Baptism and the Lord's Supper: *By His Word and command!*

Before we leave this brief discussion of the Sabbath, I want to call attention to Martin Luther's thinking that astounded me upon close examination. In His *Large Catechism* he discusses the meaning of the Ten Commandments. In dealing with the Sabbath commandment, he bases his argument in support of Sunday observance not on Biblical evidence but on tradition, expedience, and the need for good order. His position is unusual in view of the fact that he advocated the *sola scriptura*, the Bible alone, principle of interpretation. But perhaps it is not so strange when we consider that Luther sought always to follow that principle in theology and life. Because no Biblical sources support the observance of the first day of the week as a holy day, Luther could not use any. He was consistent in his application of *sola scriptura*.

Luther also indicated that in his view the Sabbath commandment does not concern Christians in any literal sense, yet he does not make the identical assertion for the other nine. One finds it difficult to understand how he could make such a distinction when the Word of God itself does not do so. Following his rejection of a literal understanding of the Sabbath commandment, and his use of the argument of tradition and expediency for Sunday observance, he makes an astounding statement:

> *Since so much depends on God's Word that no holy day is sanctified without it, we must realize that God insists upon a strict observance of this commandment and will punish all who despise his Word and refuse to hear and learn it, especially at the times appointed.*[1]

If, in this statement, Luther was referring to the Biblical seventh-day Sabbath, it would have been consistent with Biblical testimony. However, since he was upholding Sunday observance, which as we have seen is a human tradition, it constitutes legalism. Luther made the commandment command what it does not command.

This is certainly no attempt to discredit Luther as a theologian and reformer. My admiration and respect for his

---

[1] *The Large Catechism*, p. 22.

contribution to Christian thought knows no bounds. Instead, I am simply pointing out the fact that Luther was capable of error in judgment, and that he lived but one lifetime which limited his grasp of the totality of Bible truth. What he uncovered was needed in his time, and we are the beneficiaries. But we have also learned much more of Scripture since Luther. One is tempted to conjecture that, had he lived long enough, he may have recognized the need for Sabbath reformation. Present Biblical interpretation and theology have a good foundation in Luther and the other sixteenth-century reformers. But if such theology is to be true to *sola scriptura* rather than *sola Luther*, it cannot allow him to have the last word.

During the time when I was investigating the Sabbath, I prayed constantly, asking for enlightenment and guidance. One morning as I was reading in the Psalms I came to this passage:

> *I will run in the way of thy commandments when thou enlargest my understanding! Teach me, O Lord, the way of thy statutes; and I will keep it to the end. Give me understanding, that I may keep thy law and observe it with my whole heart. (Psalm 119:32-34)*

THE LORD'S SUPPER

Another aspect of Seventh-day Adventist theology that attracted my interest was its teaching on the Lord's Supper. First Corinthians 11 indicates that Christ is present in the celebration of communion. It does not suggest the transubstantiation doctrine long held by Roman Catholicism. However, it is clear that in some sense Christ is truly present when communion is celebrated. The major reformers, especially Luther and Calvin, though they differed somewhat in their explanations of the manner of His presence, agreed on this point.

Of course I wondered about the Adventist interpretation of the Lord's Supper. In one of the courses I took at the SDA Theological Seminary, I had the opportunity to compare the theology of Martin Luther, John Calvin, Ulrich Zwingli, and the Adventist writer Ellen G. White, on the Lord's Supper. To my delight I discovered that Ellen G. White's view contained elements of the thinking of these three reformation giants (and of John Wesley who appeared somewhat later). Her most complete statement appears in chapter 72 of her classical volume *Desire of Ages.*

She speaks of the Lord's Supper as a "memorial" of Christ's sacrifice, which parallels Calvin's concept. Her counsel that in partaking of the Communion the believer's attention must be on the cross of Christ also reminds one of Calvin's thought. Beholding the love of Christ, the Christian will be "elevated in thought, purified in heart, transformed in character." In other words, something of a spiritual and inner nature happens to the one who communes in faith. The experience of communion is not just objective but subjective as well.

Her statement on the bread and wine, "These emblems Christ employs to *represent* His own unblemished sacrifice," portrays a position similar to that of Zwingli.[2]

Agreeing with Luther that Christ is really present in the celebration of the Lord's Supper, she writes:

> *With hearts cleansed by Christ's most precious blood, in full consciousness of His presence, although unseen, they are to hear His words, "Peace I leave with you, my peace I give unto you: not as the world gives, give I unto you." (John 14:27 KJV.)*

A number of times she refers to the Supper as a sacrament. Because she saw the Lord's Supper as sacramental in nature, that is to say, God himself acting and at work in the celebration, she could say in words similar to those of Luther, "Hearts and hands that are unworthy may even administer the ordinance, yet Christ is there to minister to His children." She recognizes that because in the sacrament of the Lord's Supper the believers "come to meet with Christ," the giving and receiving of its blessings are not contingent upon the personal character of the officiating clergymen or local elders.

However, like Luther and Calvin, Ellen. G. White recognized the role of faith in receiving the blessing of the Lord's Supper. She said: "As faith contemplates our Lord's great sacrifice, the soul assimilates the spiritual life of Christ. That soul will receive spiritual strength from every communion." What is received by faith in the celebration of

---

[2] Emphasis supplied.

the Lord's Supper is not only additional cognitive and objective understanding of revelation, but also the subjective assimilation of the spiritual life of Christ. Thus the believer who comes in faith receives spiritual strength from every communion.

"To the death of Christ we owe even this earthly life," she said. The breadth of her sacramental view is revealed in the following breathtaking statement:

> *The bread we eat is the purchase of His broken body. The water we drink is bought by His spilled blood. Never one, saint or sinner, eats his daily food, but he is nourished by the body and blood of Christ. The cross of Calvary is stamped on every loaf. It is reflected in every water spring. . . . The family board becomes as the table of the Lord, and every meal a sacrament.*

Such a view of the Lord's Supper, a beautiful union of the best eucharistic theology of the Reformation, indicates the spiritual richness that exists in the life of the Seventh-day Adventist Church. One should expect that the last-day church would have a total grasp and understanding of Biblical faith and life.

BAPTISM

During my studies at Andrews University the faculty was most gracious in making themselves available for special dialogues. Our meetings took place on Wednesday evenings and covered a wide range of topics of my own choosing. The only stipulation was that the professors involved would know the topic to be discussed a week in advance.

One of the topics discussed was baptism. I was particularly interested in knowing if the Seventh-day Adventist Church held to what is known in some denominations as "believer's baptism," or did they hold a view in which God was active in baptism. In other words was baptism seen only as a human act, a public witness to a prior conversion experience, or was God acting in the baptismal celebration?

Baptism viewed only as a human act is often revealed during the baptismal ritual when the pastor says words such as: "Because you have received Christ as your personal

Saviour, I baptize you...." This most frequently used baptismal formula represents a decidedly anthropocentric, humanistic, perception of the Christian religion. Whereas baptism viewed both as an act of God, and as a public witness, is revealed in the ritual when the pastor says words similar to:

> *Because Jesus Christ has come into your life and made you His own possession; because He has forgiven your sins by means of His Word and the ministry of the Holy Spirit, and you have accepted His forgiveness by faith, I therefore baptize you....*

This baptismal formula represents a more theocentric perception of the Christian religion, a perception to which contemporary Christians need to return. The focus is not only on what humans do in religion, but more importantly on what God does by His grace.

That Seventh-day Adventists believe God acts in baptism, that it is more than a human witness to conversion, was pointed out to me on one of those Wednesday evenings when the following theocentric passage by Ellen G. White was read:

> *Let those who received the imprint of God by baptism [remember] that upon them the Lord has placed His signature, declaring them to be His sons and daughters.*[3]

For the Seventh-day Adventist Church baptism is an act of God's grace and an act of human faith and surrender.[4]

---

[3] *Seventh-day Adventist Bible Commentary*, Vol. 6, p. 1075.

[4] For a more complete discussion of the sacraments within Adventism see my book *Sing A New Song!* (Berrien Springs, Michigan: Andrews University Press, 1984), pp. 60-86.

10

MEET MRS. WHITE

Although I had heard of Ellen G. White many years prior to Shirley's decision to unite with the Seventh-day Adventist Church, I never made any assessment of her. However, when I learned that Adventists believe she possessed the gift of prophecy and that her writings are valuable counsel, I rebelled. It was not that I questioned the reality of the prophetic gift, simply that she had it.

I thought my wife had lost her spiritual equilibrium completely when she began poring over Mrs. White's books. She read *The Great Controversy*, *The Desire of Ages*, *The Acts of the Apostles*, and many others during 1968-69. During 1970 she read all the *Testimonies*.

BIOGRAPHICAL SKETCH

I anticipated that the role of Ellen G. White would be the most difficult aspect of Adventism to understand and accept. In fact, I was totally prepared to reject out of hand the entire idea of Mrs. White exercising the prophetic gift. That is, until I made an investigation of my own.

For the benefit of non-Adventist readers, it might prove helpful to give a brief biographical sketch of Mrs. White.

She was born, a twin, on November 26, 1827, on a farm near Gorham, Maine. Her parents, Robert and Eunice Harmon, were farmers until they moved to Portland, Maine, where her father opened a small business to support his family of eight children. Ellen was a very active youngster, known for her cheerfulness and helpfulness both at home and at her father's hat factory. As she returned home from school one day at the age of nine, a stone thrown by a schoolmate injured her badly. The blow on the bridge of the nose left her unconscious for three weeks. From that time on, her health fluctuated. It is somewhat miraculous that she accomplished so much in adult life and lived to the age of 87.

As a result of that accident, she was unable to continue her schoolwork. In the summer of 1840 Ellen and her parents attended a Methodist campmeeting. There the twelve-year old girl responded to the Gospel and surrendered her life to God. In 1842 a Methodist minister baptized her by immersion, and on June 26 she became a member of the Methodist Church. Prior to this, however, her family attended religious meetings in Portland, Maine, during which they accepted the views of an itinerant preacher and evangelist by the name of William Miller. Together with many others they began to hope for Christ's soon return.

Ellen Harmon became an enthusiastic and capable missionary for Christ and the message of His second coming. Often she would deprive herself of some of life's comforts in order to have the material means to purchase tracts for evangelism.

In late December, 1844, a critical time for the Millerite believers in the return of Christ, she was visiting a friend in Portland, Maine. While there seventeen-year-old Ellen experienced the first of many visions from the Lord. In that initial vision she saw symbolized the triumphant arrival of the Adventist believers in the City of God.

Reluctantly she told of the vision to her friends. All accepted it as light from God. Their hope began to renew. The late 1840's and the 1850's were difficult days for the early Adventists. They met with much scoffing and ridicule, much of it aimed at Ellen Harmon because of her visions. Among themselves they struggled with disunity, which resulted in fanaticism tearing them even further apart.

In subsequent visions Ellen received instruction to counter the fanaticism and reprove wrong and doctrinal error. It was a very difficult task for such a young girl in the face of the disbelief toward her visions and prejudice because of her age. It is not difficult to understand the skepticism with which many viewed Ellen Harmon. It is wise to be careful about such a phenomenon. The Bible itself counsels caution. But the Bible also urges us to test claims of prophecy to see if they are from God. We cannot find

84

out if something is true or false unless we examine the evidence. We must commend the early Adventist pioneers who, in spite of their initial disbelief and skepticism, tested her gift.

On a number of occasions men and women witnessed Ellen as she experienced the gift. Many of them were respected Christians and citizens whose accounts have been carefully documented and preserved.[1] After cautious investigation and firsthand observation of Ellen in vision, the early Adventists accepted her gift and heeded her counsel. Her guidance proved invaluable in the formative years of the Seventh-day Adventist Church.

Critics of the Seventh-day Adventist Church assert that it has based its theology on Ellen G. White's visions. Nothing could be further from the truth. While Adventists believe her counsel to be inspired and revere and trust it, the theology and doctrines of the Church come from the Bible. A careful and unprejudiced study of Adventist history reveals the formulation of particular doctrines often years before she had a vision relative to it.

The crucial test of doctrine and spiritual life is whether or not Christ is glorified. On virtually every page of Ellen G. White's voluminous writings she presents and extols Christ. Constantly she calls attention to the Word of God and pleads for the reader to believe and practice it. Her severest contemporary critic, D. M. Canright, a former friend and Adventist minister, cites a number of quotations to suggest that she played up herself, but after careful checking, I found that she did not glorify herself as he suggests. The original context of the statements Canright quotes prove otherwise.

In August, 1846, Ellen Harmon and James White united in marriage. By 1860 the family numbered six with the addition of four boys. Poverty and distress were daily companions in their early years, and James White had to do some farming to supplement his meager income as a traveling preacher.

---

[1] Detailed information can be obtained from the *Ellen G. White Estate Office*, 6840 Eastern Ave., NW, Washington, D. C. 20012, or the *Ellen G. White Estate Branch Office*, Andrews University, Berrien Springs, MI 49104.

Mrs. White's first book was published in 1851. In 1855 the family moved to Battle Creek, Michigan, to help reestablish the Adventist publishing organization. The next few years the White's spent traveling to help consolidate the young but growing denomination.

The White family did not escape tragedy and suffering. Henry, the first-born, died at the age of sixteen. Another son, Herbert, died in infancy. James himself died in Battle Creek on August 6, 1881. Ellen suffered periodic bouts with illness. It was as though the Lord employed such means to keep her humble and dependent in using the unusual gift He had given her.

Ellen White wrote thirty-nine major books during her lifetime, was co-author for three, and prepared countless articles for denominational publications. In addition, many compilations of her original books and articles have been prepared by the Church. In spite of a meager education, her special gift enabled her to have immense influence in motivating and inspiring the proclamation of the Sabbath, new health practices, the second coming of Christ, and the particular mission of the Adventist Church. She was instrumental in founding institutions of learning and of health care and wrote much for the periodical, *The Advent Review and Sabbath Herald.* Her work took her to Europe from 1885 to 1887, where she visited Switzerland, England, Germany, France, Italy, Denmark, Norway, and Sweden.

In December, 1891, she arrived in Australia, and her visit resulted in the founding of Avondale College as well as the Australian medical missionary program. In 1900 she returned to the U.S.A. to live in St. Helena, California. The last fifteen years of her life were spent in writing and travel to fulfill speaking appointments. In 1909 Ellen White made her last appearance at a General Conference session of the Seventh-day Adventist Church. Her final illness began when on Sabbath morning, February 13, 1915, she fell while entering her study. For five months she was confined to bed or wheelchair. At the age of eighty-seven the remarkable life of a great woman came to a quiet end. She lies buried beside her husband in the Oak Hill Cemetery in Battle Creek, Michigan. No great monument marks the spot. The family plot contains an unostentatious central stone inscribed with the names of all those buried there, and her own resting place is marked with a simple stone engraved with one word: MOTHER.

Throughout her service to the Adventist Church she consistently refused all elective offices as well as ordination. She did not need to be ordained in order to perform the particular ministry to which she was called by the Lord. But she was accorded such respect and admiration by the denomination's leaders that they generally heeded her counsel on vital matters. Experience had led to trust in her wisdom.

PROTECTIVE ROLE

To be sure, it is difficult to conceive of someone contemporary having the gift of prophecy. But we cannot ignore it. We must put the gift to the test so that it either authenticates or condemns itself. By their fruits we shall know them, counsels the Word of God. Mrs. White's lifetime work resulted in harmony of faith and doctrine among Adventist believers, and the fantastic growth of the Adventist Church. Thousands of individuals will testify how she has helped them come to a vivid experience of knowing Jesus Christ; know Him, not just know about Him. She has been, and continues to be, a spiritual friend to many devout believers in Christ. Her little book *Steps to Christ* is one of the best expositions of the way of salvation ever written.

Upon her death, tributes poured in from around the world. Churchmen and non-churchmen alike recognized her as a great figure and a powerful influence for good in her time. The passage of years has proved the accuracy of many of her counsels on health and education. Today we recognize the harmful effects of tobacco, alcohol, and drugs, which she warned against in her time. She suggested that a germ caused cancer. Medical researchers today have concluded it to be a virus-induced disease. She warned of the hazard to health of eating animal fat, confirmed by research today regarding the role of cholesterol in some coronary diseases. Countless people around the world, then and now, have adopted the vegetarian diet she espoused. Since time has proven her right on such things, the obvious question is: Could she be right about other things as well?

Seventh-day Adventists do not believe that Mrs. White had a canonical mission. That is to say, God never intended that her writings be added to Scripture so as to enlarge the Bible. Nor were Adventists to take them as equal to the Bible. However, Adventists do welcome and receive them as inspired counsel and as inspired commentary on the Word of

God. She spoke of her writings as a "lesser light" pointing to the "greater light."

What God has communicated to man, we must take seriously. That prophecy is one of the spiritual gifts God gives to His church we cannot deny. (1 Corinthians 12:1-31; 14:1-25; Ephesians 4:11-16.) The Bible states its functions as "building up the body of Christ." It helps develop mature faith so that the "cunning of men" might not sway the church, especially the church of the last days.

In the writings of Mrs. White, which certainly earn her credit as a spiritual theologian of the first rank, we find a beautifully consistent interpretation of the Word of God. An interpretation which has as its apex and center the person of Jesus Christ. In every doctrine that Mrs. White wrote about she glorified Him and presents Him to the world as the Saviour. Righteousness by the grace of God through faith in Him is her basic theme just as it was with Luther, Calvin, and the other great Reformers of the sixteenth century.

The pulpit of the Seventh-day Adventist Tabernacle Church in Battle Creek, Michigan, has inscribed on it the words, "Sir, we would see Jesus." There is no more eloquent testimony to the Christ-centered legacy of Ellen G. White.

What relationship do her writings have with Bible study and developing theology within Seventh-day Adventism? In other words, do her writings prohibit or inhibit further study and insight?

Mrs. White's role in the development of Adventist theology has been one of guidance and direction. Such guidance has been fortunate, especially during the decades following World War I, which saw the emergence of theological liberalism on the European continent. It has also protected the Adventist Church in America during the decades following World War II from the seeds of ecumenism sown in the late twenties and thirties. A theology antagonistic to evangelism and conversion, as the primary task and goal of the Christian church, has fertilized the growth of ecumenism. Ecumenical theology has led to the abandonment of the historic relationship between God's law and God's gospel. It has also created misunderstanding of the nature of Christian freedom.

To be sure, Christ has set us free, but not free to live as we please. He freed us by His sacrifice and power from those things which hinder us from living in an obedient relationship to Him: namely, the power of Satan, the power of sin, and the power of the flesh. Liberated from the power of these, we are free to live as He directs and are enabled to do so by His Holy Spirit. Mrs. White's writings and teachings have maintained, upheld, and spread to all who will listen the fundamental elements of God's revelation and plan of salvation despite the religious liberalism of the twentieth century. That, in my view, has been one of her major contributions to contemporary Christianity and to the Adventist Church in particular.

The road to Biblical study and investigation is wide open and stretches before the Adventist Church. The writings of Ellen G. White do not constitute a barricade across the road of Biblical studies and theological scholarship. Rather, they constitute a fence along both sides of the road of such inquiry to protect the church from veering away from the straight and narrow of God's revelation. That purpose of her work must always be maintained by Adventists.

Seventh-day Adventists firmly believe that the Bible has ultimate authority. The writings of Ellen G. White serve in a unique way to point to the Bible as the only reliable and authentic source for faith and life. One of the professors at the SDA Theological Seminary often described Adventist theology as *nove-non-nova*--new light, not new truth.

God will utilize the work of Mrs. White to assist in the completion of the great reformation begun by Martin Luther in the sixteenth century. The major difference between Luther and Ellen G. White has to do with the manner by which God spoke through them. Luther proclaimed God's Word to his age after much intellectual wrestling with the Biblical message. Mrs. White proclaims God's Word in our day after having received instruction by means of vision. The spirit of both is the same: the Spirit of Jesus Christ!

It is my conviction that in the closing days of earth's history God will restore all of the spiritual gifts to the worship and life of the faithful church. It was not at all difficult for me to accept Mrs. White's role and the authenticity and reliability of her counsel. How was it possible? By setting aside my skepticism and putting her gift to the test. I simply read as much as possible of her writings. Truth is truth. The Spirit of Christ is the Spirit of Christ. Read her books, and you will discover that fact for yourself. They may convict you, may disturb you, may even anger you in their portrayal of the condition of your heart and life.

But they will also bring you to the foot of Christ's cross and apply its healing balm to your repentant and confessing heart, as they did to mine.

Meet Mrs. White! She will help you to know Jesus Christ, become more like Him, and get ready for His second advent.

11

VOWS AND VICTORIES

Webster's New Collegiate Dictionary defines a vow as a "solemn promise, especially one made to God or to some deity; an act by which one consecrates or devotes himself to some act, service, or condition." After becoming a Christian, I made two such vows.

WEDDING AND ORDINATION

The first vow was made at the marriage altar, where I pledged to love, honor, and keep my wife in sickness or in health, for better or for worse, until death. The second vow was made upon ordination into the Christian ministry, both made, incidentally, on the twenty-fifth of June. My marriage vow was made on June 25, 1955, and my ordination vow on June 25, 1961.

June 25, 1961, was an unforgettable day. It will always represent the point in time when I was set apart for the ministry. I have tried to be faithful to the pledge I made on that day. The ordination service took place in Fairport Harbor, Ohio, amid the solemnity of the annual convention of the Finnish Evangelical Lutheran Church. It was a most impressive service, which Shirley and I remember with nostalgia. The sermon, preached by the president of the church, challenged the four of us to be ordained to faithfulness in the work of the ministry. It made me extremely conscious of the historicity and perpetuity of the church of Jesus Christ, as well as of the gifts God chooses to give His church, one of which is the ordained ministry. The pastor of my home congregation, St Mark's Lutheran Church, Waukegan, Illinois, gave me the ministerial charge, then the moment of public avowal came. The presiding officer addressed us as we stood before him and the assembled congregation:

> *As you shall give account before the Lord in the great day of His appearing, and that this congregation here present may know your mind and will in these, I call upon you now to make answer before Almighty God: Are you now ready to take upon you this holy ministry, and faithfully to serve therein?*

Each of us answered in turn: "Yes, by the help of God."

"Will you preach and teach the Word of God in accordance with the confessions of the church, and will you administer the holy sacraments after the ordinance of Christ?"

"Yes, by the help of God," we each answered.

"Will you be diligent in the study of Holy Scripture, instant in prayer, and faithful in the use of the means of grace?"

"Yes, by the help of God."

"Will you adorn the doctrine of God our Saviour by a holy life and conversation?"

"Yes, by the help of God."

Each of us then concluded with the solemn pledge:

> *Before God, and the Lord Jesus, who shall judge the quick and the dead at His appearing, I do promise, with His grace and help, to fulfill these sacred obligations. Amen.*

We then knelt and by the laying on of hands the office of the pastoral ministry was declared conferred in the name of the triune God. A most serious moment, it represented a binding vow. Little did I know then that the two vows made on June 25, six years apart, would be inextricably combined in a great crisis ten years later.

VOW'S INTENT

While I continued to investigate Adventist theology and life-style, my ordination vow loomed up from the past. It prohibited me from rushing headlong into the Seventh-day Adventist Church until I knew what it would involve. For

92

that I am grateful. Over and over again I asked myself the question: "What about my ordination vow? Does it bind me to the Lutheran Church?"

As I slowly grasped the truth of Seventh-day Adventism, it was necessary to carefully analyze the content and intent of my ordination vow. A number of things became immediately apparent. First, though I accepted the holy ministry in the context of the Lutheran Church, I had made the vow to God and not to the Lutheran Church. It was the holy ministry I accepted, not just the Lutheran pastorate.

Second, the vow concerned preaching and teaching the Word of God in accordance with the Lutheran confessions of the sixteenth century. I understood that to mean *insofar* as the confessions were true and accurate interpretations of the Word of God. Thus I did not, and could not, adhere to them in the same manner as to the Word of God.

Third, the vow called for a diligent study of Holy Scripture. It obligated me to search out the deep meanings and truths of the Bible so as to teach them to my people. I believed Lutheran preaching and teaching to be Biblical preaching and teaching. That is to say, truth must be proclaimed according to Luther's principle of *sola scriptura.*

Fourth, the pledge involved faithfulness in the use of the *means of grace*, the ways God offers salvation to mankind. These included not only baptism and the Lord's supper, but also the preaching office which declares the Word of God.

Fifth, the vow included the promise of holiness of life and conversation. I, as pastor and preacher, must seek to practice God's truth in my own life as a true leader and shepherd of the people of God.

Slowly but steadily during my stay at Andrews University, I began to realize that in order to remain faithful to my ordination vow I must continue to study the Scripture, and when I discovered truth apply it to my life. To examine thoroughly the theology of the Seventh-day Adventist Church, and to accept it should it be proven true, was in fact being faithful to my ordination vow.

By my vow I had placed myself under obligation to study the Scriptures, to remain open to new light, new insight from its pages. The mandate to dig deeper was mine, and in so doing I honored my vow before God. When and if the Bible should reveal new light I must proclaim and spread it. The privilege exists to reject new knowledge and to suffer the consequences. But when new light is seen and accepted, there is an immediate compulsion to share it with as many as will listen.

Another aspect of faithfulness to my ordination vow also commanded my attention. The vow was made to God. I pledged faithfulness to Him and to His Word. At times such faithfulness may require change. Faithfulness to God and faithfulness to a denomination are not necessarily synonymous. At times one may have to choose between the two. That is to say, if the denomination is no longer completely loyal to God and to His Word, then the individual must follow God. Luther had to make such a choice. God is protecting His church by calling His faithful ones apart from following mere tradition, be it ancient or modern, to a deeper surrender to Biblical principle.

The Christian owes allegiance only to God. No person owes loyalty to any denomination because of what it may have once stood for, but must follow God and His truth. There, and there alone, is spiritual safety, a point I had to consider as I compared the theology of the Seventh-day Adventist Church with prevailing Lutheran and contemporary Protestant theology. I also viewed what I learned at the SDA Theological Seminary in the light of the contemporary ecumenical movement. To my amazement I discovered that the Seventh-day Adventist Church represented the true ecumenical movement as part of its mission is to call all God's people to a unity based on Scripture. This is in stark contrast to the world ecumenical movement which seeks to join churches on the basis of compromise.

SATISFYING THEOLOGY

As my study continued it became apparent that I could be more faithful to God, and my ordination vow, within the Adventist Church. It became a matter of building upon rather than of abandoning something. The Lutheran heritage still remains a vital part of me and always will. It was a source of great pleasure to discover with what respect the Seventh-day Adventist Church holds the contribution of Martin Luther.

Respecting a heritage is one thing. Permitting it to judge the Word of God is another. The Bible must mold the heritage, not the other way around. This helped me to discover a more satisfying theology of the relationship between the law and gospel in Adventism. Adventism has insisted that the Bible be its own interpreter. Generally speaking, Protestant theology today has tended to hold the Old and New testaments in tension, in an antithetical relationship. The view is that the New Testament effectively cancels out the Old except for matters of historical significance. The Old Testament is seen as standing for God's law while the New Testament stands for His grace. Thus the Bible appears irreconcilable and contradictory, the inevitable consequence of discarding God's law as a valid influence in the believer's life.

Martin Luther and John Calvin held that God's law has three basic functions: (1) a civil use as a norm for social law and order, (2) a religious use to convict of sin and drive the sinner to Christ, (3) an ethical norm for the obedient Christian life, obeyed out of love and gratitude for the gift of salvation. The current view drops the law as guide and substitutes the Holy Spirit.

Many now assert that the believer must follow the Holy Spirit alone. That the Christian must accept the Holy Spirit's leading we dare not deny. But the Holy Spirit is the Spirit of truth. He will never guide the believer contrary to the revealed Word of God. The Holy Spirit will never work in the mind and conscience apart from, or in contradiction to, the written Word. The Spirit will assuredly lead into all truth, but it will be the truth of the Word of God. Only thus do we have assurance that what the Spirit reveals is in fact God's truth.

The Old and New Testaments are not antithetical. They are in harmony. Therefore, we must reject the view that the gospel has canceled God's law. Both His law and His gospel of salvation in Christ are part of His grace. Both law and gospel work in harmony to bring the sinner to faith in Christ, and then to keep the forgiven sinner on the straight and narrow way of sanctification.

Anyone who wants to grasp Seventh-day Adventist theology must comprehend these two opposing points of view. It is also basic to a correct understanding of the nature of the faith life. The Old and New Testaments do not oppose each other, but bear witness to a revelation that progresses toward the incarnation of the Son of God and triumphs in His second advent.

Passages in the Pauline epistles do indicate that the believer in Christ is no longer under the law. Critics often use Galatians 3:23-25 as proof that Christ's coming has completely canceled the law as far as the believer is concerned. But it doesn't say that. Nowhere does Paul suggest that Christ did away with the law. In fact, he insists that the new life of faith establishes and upholds the law which is holy and good. (Romans 3:31; 7:12.) He also indicates that those who keep the law will be those who are justified (Romans 2:13), that is, the justified will observe the law.

The Bible clearly teaches that the person who accepts Christ as Saviour will have a changed life. Conversion effects no change in the law of God or in its function and claim upon the Christian. Change will take place, however, by the power of the Holy Spirit, *within the believer* in such a way that God's law is no longer disregarded. Rather, the converted person comes into harmony with it. When a person has the right relationship with Christ, a right relationship with the law of God is also established. The Christian wills what God wills. He wants what God wants. He sees the law not as a hateful and impossible burden, but as a welcome and glorious revelation of God's desire and plan for holiness of life.

Without faith in Christ an individual stands under the dominion, power, and curse of the law. But by faith in Christ that person comes into harmony with the law of God because Christ is the fulfiller of that law. To be in Christ is to desire the righteousness of life which God reveals in His law. Jesus Christ has set the believer free from the power of Satan and sin so that it becomes possible in fact to please God by living in harmony with His law. It is the power of the indwelling Holy Spirit which makes this faith/obedience possible for the believer.

Apart from faith in Christ it is impossible to keep the Ten Commandments. But with Christ all things are possible. In Christ God has made provision for us to keep His law. If we surrender our lives to Christ, He will come in and fill us with His holiness. The Christian does not have to sin anymore. The sinful nature still remains, but the redeemed person does not have to commit sin. By the power of the Holy Spirit the Christian can live without sinning. But if sin is committed, due to the weakness of sinful nature, there is an advocate with the Father (1 John 1:8-2:2).

The question for the believer then is not, "Am I keeping the law?" but rather, "Am I abiding in Christ, and

He in me?" Christ fulfilled and kept the law perfectly, and continues to do so when He dwells within the believer. Thus, if He dwells within you, and His Holy Spirit reveals the truth about the seventh-day Sabbath, you will observe that day because Jesus kept it and still does. Is it possible to keep God's law? By ourselves, No! With Christ abiding in us, Yes! Attempted apart from Christ, it is impossible. If, as Paul says, all things are possible through Christ, so is the keeping of God's law.

The Sermon on the Mount records Christ's own attitude toward God's law:

> *Think not that I have come to abolish the law and the prophets; I have come not to abolish them but to fulfil them. For truly, I say to you, till heaven and earth pass away, not an iota, not a dot, will pass from the law until all is accomplished. Whoever then relaxes one of the least of these commandments and teaches men so, shall be called least in the kingdom of heaven; but he who does them and teaches them shall be called great in the kingdom of heaven. (Matthew 5:17-19)*

Obviously our Lord was referring to far more than His own words of instruction in His reference to the law and the prophets. He indicates the existence of God's law until at least the creation of the new heaven and earth. Then He impresses upon us the seriousness with which we must view the teaching of God's law. We must not relax or weaken God's commandments one bit, nor must we encourage others to do so. On the contrary, by word and example, God's people--and in particular His spiritual shepherds--must uphold and uplift God's commandments before the world. It is, therefore, a serious matter for a minister of the gospel to understand and teach the proper relationship between law and gospel. God does not command the impossible. With the command He offers the grace which makes obedience possible.

Assurance of salvation springs from trust in God. The prodigal son was not certain of his father's love, and of his own sonship, until he returned home and accepted his father's love.

When the prodigal son returned home, his father did not give him the third degree. The father did not ask where he had been and what he had done. He only cared that his lost son came home! Welcoming him, he kissed him, and called for a feast of celebration. Can we assume that the son, having returned home, having been received by his father, now lived in his father's house with the same rebellious attitude that led him to leave it earlier? Isn't it far more realistic to assume that in acceptance of his father's love and generosity, and in obedience to his father, he found his freedom and assurance of sonship?

God has a right to command His children, because He is God. The Bible calls the church the body of Christ and refers to Him as its head. The head of the body has something to say about how the body functions.

When my son David was young one of his responsibilities was taking out the garbage. I recall him going off to do his chore whistling or humming. Did that simple task cause an awareness of sonship with his father? I think it did, because when he happily whistled down the stairs with his clumsy burden, it was not because of his joy at lugging a pail of garbage, but from the privilege of doing something his father wanted done. For him, disposing of the garbage was an honorable responsibility. It somehow assured him of his sonship and belonging in the family. As a child he may not have realized what it was about his task that made him feel happy. But I think he knew that pleasing the father he loved, and who he knew loved him, gave him great joy.

My son did not obey to gain my love. He already knew he was loved. To obey in order to earn love is legalism and only frustrates. One is never certain the obedience is enough. But to obey in response to love is something entirely different. Love gives confidence. Even when my little son stumbled, fell, and scattered garbage everywhere, he knew from my continued love that I understood he was doing his best. My forgiving and understanding love motivated him to continue to obey.

This is the kind of relationship we can have with our heavenly Father. Just as a child is happiest and most content when in a relationship of loving obedience with father and mother, the same is true in our relationship with God. We obey Him not to earn sonship, but to exercise it. That's why Jesus said, "If you love me, you will keep my commandments." (John 14:15) No one who persistently and willfully disobeys God's clear will can be sure of the relationship with God. "And by this we may be sure that we know him, if we keep his commandments." (1 John 2:3) "We may" is followed by "if we." One can know he is God's child if by faith he desires to follow God's commandments.

One point must be kept clearly in mind. I can no more perfectly obey my Father's commandments than my son obeyed mine. My failure to do so could cause me grave anxiety about my place in God's affections except for the fact that it is not dependant upon what I do, but on His forgiving and encouraging love. When I realize this, it motivates me to desire perfect obedience despite my imperfections. A major way of responding to God's love is to long to reflect the standard of Christ's own character, His law. As the personalities of two people in love come to resemble each other, so a person's growing love for Christ makes that person want to become like Him.

The prodigal had to meet certain conditions in order to live in his father's house, the major one being that he must yield to the fact that the father was the father. The person who claims to be a Christian must decide whether he wants to keep God's commandments or not. That decision is critical for the maintenance of the relationship. Love for God is perfected when His people love His Word and want to keep it.

When the believer looks to the cross of Christ the sacrificial extent of God's love is so obvious. What else can be done than obey the One who loves us so much?

There are two great symbols of conflict and victory in the Bible: the empty tomb and the empty cross. Jesus Christ died on the cross for the world's sin, for yours and mine. He was buried in a cold tomb and raised from the dead. He is now neither on the cross nor in the tomb! He is in the heavenly sanctuary in the role of High Priest and He is with us by His Spirit. And the Word of God can say, "All who keep his commandments abide in him, and he in them." (1 John 3:24)

VICTORY!

I learned much about Adventist beliefs. One can either use knowledge or ignore it. A response was required. Decision time came in March 1971. At the end of the winter quarter my little daughter Rhoda and I drove to Destin, Florida. I wanted to be alone, away from all Lutherans and all Adventists, in order to weigh the evidence without influence either way.

A kind friend of my parents, who belonged to an independent community church, had invited Rhoda and me to Destin. I knew that friend would have no vested interests in my decision and accepted the invitation.

Shirley understood my need to be alone as I struggled with one of the most important and decisive decisions of my life. Can you imagine what her feelings were like as I left for Florida? Can you imagine how she prayed during my absence? The outcome would affect her future too.

On the white sand beach of the Gulf Coast I pondered and prayed, weighed the evidence and compared the theology and life-style of the two churches: Lutheran and Adventist. Anticipating that the decision would be difficult to make, I discovered it wasn't. All of the historical, Biblical, and practical evidence I assessed favored the Seventh-day Adventist Church. When I explained to my host the reason for the trip, and for my decision, she remarked, "Your choice was obvious. God has been leading you." From such an unexpected source came immediate confirmation of my decision.

In faithfulness to my marriage and ordination vows I found victory in the greatest crisis of my Christian life. However, I do not want to give the impression that I never knew the nature of the Christian faith before my experience at Andrews University. It was not a matter of conversion. I had been a Christian for many years, so it was a matter of exposure to new insight and a crystallization of other convictions long held.

Arriving back in Berrien Springs, I sent a letter of resignation to the headquarters of the Lutheran Church in America. Following the acceptance of my resignation, and based upon my study of Adventist theology, I was baptized by immersion by Dr. Thomas Blincoe at Pioneer Memorial Church, on the campus of Andrews University, on April 24, 1971.

With spiritual unity restored, Shirley was no longer a stranger in my home. The gulf that had separated us vanished. Once again our lives were united in a common hope and purpose.

12

THE CHURCH IN
PROPHETIC PERSPECTIVE

What kind of Church did I join? Where does the Seventh-day Adventist Church fit in the spectrum of Christian churches? Perhaps it can best be explained by first viewing the SDA Church in an historical perspective.

FOUR EPOCHS

For the sake of this narrative, the history of the Christian church is viewed in terms of four general epochs. The first, from the time of the apostles to the latter part of the second century A.D., comprised the period of the early church. Paul's epistles helped shape its doctrines, and his travels spread Christianity across the then-known world. It was a period of growth, of struggle and of persecution. Doctrinal heresies, mostly involving the person of Christ, racked the young church. Church leaders saw the need to formulate creeds, and a form of church government began to evolve which completely changed the church from its original condition.

The second epoch extends from the end of the second century to the second decade of the sixteenth century. It witnessed the development and establishment of the power of bishops and the gradual supremacy of the bishop of Rome. The church learned to express the Biblical picture of God as the Trinity of Father, Son, and Holy Spirit. Theologians settled the relationship of Christ to the Father at the Council of Nicea in A.D. 325. The worship of Mary, the mother of God, as the first among saints gained credence.

101

The doctrine of transubstantiation in the Lord's Supper, together with the concept of the mass, emerged. The concepts of purgatory and penance grew rapidly.

The second epoch was also a period of papal and church involvement in the political affairs of a growing number of developing nations and empires. The entanglements of such involvement eventually led to a controversy over the papal throne, which resulted in the move of the papacy to Avignon, France, in 1309. Actually, two popes ruled part of the time, one in France and the other in Italy, each condemning the other. That schism was one of Christendom's greatest scandals. In November, 1417, the Council of Constance ended that schism, but never again would the papacy enjoy the power and prestige it once possessed. The office of the pope changed from that of an absolute to a constitutional monarch. Still, subsequent popes sought to regain the papacy's former power and splendor.

The third epoch began with the great Protestant reformation of the sixteenth century. Yet its roots go farther back. A strong desire for learning was part of the Renaissance of the previous century. In Germany alone no fewer than twelve universities were established between 1409 and 1506. A brand of theology and philosophy called "humanism" appeared as a by-product of the Renaissance. Humanism represented a shift in intellectual thought from the supernatural and transcendent to what was considered characteristically human, the ability of man's reason. Many of the humanists were religiously minded, however, and played an instrumental role in preparing the way for the reformation. They restudied the Christian sources and approached life in a new way which sought to release the mind from the shackles of traditionalism. The greatest religious humanist was Desiderius Erasmus, whose influence had its strongest impact during Martin Luther's lifetime. Though he freely criticized the superstition and corruption of the Roman Catholic Church, his views did not lead to a break with the church. Luther was a different kind of man. God used him, together with Philipp Melanchthon, John Calvin, Ulrich Zwingli, and others, to restore to the world the gospel of justification by grace through faith. The Protestant churches which grew from their teaching became mighty evangelistic forces. After a lengthy period of theological consolidation in the various Protestant denominations, a zeal for missionary outreach developed.

The fourth epoch began with the archbishopric of Nathan Soderblom, of the Lutheran Church in Sweden (1914-1931). Enthusiastic for Christian unity, he became the major organizer of the first ecumenical conference of Protestants, held in Stockholm in 1925. Since then there has been a great campaign for the reunification of Christian denominations that remains undiminished to this day. Many denominational churches of the same confession have united to form new church bodies. A positive by-product of the ecumenical movement is that Christians of differing religious backgrounds are learning to know and appreciate one another. On the negative side, there has been the watering down of the Protestant theological heritage in order to make union more attractive and possible. Anglicans are drawing closer to Rome, and Lutherans closer to Anglicans. As a result many laymen have become confused and uncertain about the fundamental validity of ecumenicity and the position their denominations have taken toward the interpretation of Scripture. Many of them are not even aware of the trends within their church until it is too late. Some brave voices that have tried to issue warnings, such as the Presbyterian New Testament scholar Gresham Machen, have often been silenced by accusations of disloyalty and divisiveness. But the trends away from Biblical and historical Christianity are increasingly disturbing. Some people are fearful that the church will become unrecognizable as a Christian communion basing belief and life on the Bible and the Bible alone.

As the epoch of the reformation waned and the age of ecumenism began, the Seventh-day Adventist Church appeared on the scene. From inauspicious beginnings based on an interpretation of the book of Daniel in the 1840's, the Adventist movement now encompasses the world. Its missionaries and missions are far-flung. The results have been phenomenal. Around the globe membership in the five million member church increases at the rate of 1000+ per day. People are drawn to the ranks of a church which seems to know where it is headed in a world that is not so sure of its ultimate destiny. Why is this so?

TRUTH WHOSE TIME HAS COME

The following statement by LeRoy E. Froom contains the clue to the answer:

There is nothing in this old world more powerful than a Heaven-indicted truth whose time has come. No human hand can stay or deflect it. All heaven is behind its proclamation. With the coming of the appointed time both the messenger and the message are destined to appear. Some may ignore, minimize, oppose, or reject it, but its witness is bound to be borne, and to have its destined effect. If men were to fail to give it, God would summon the very rocks, as it were, to declare it. (Luke 19:40.)[1]

Critics of Adventism claim that it began in error and, therefore, continues to be untrustworthy. The opposite is in reality true. The Seventh-day Adventist Church and its theology began as a **recognition of** and **correction of** previous error. The early nineteenth-century American religious leader William Miller, examining Daniel 8:14 and related texts, came to the conclusion that the cleansing mentioned in the passage referred to the earth and the church. After careful study of the time prophecies of Daniel in relation to historical events and evidence, Miller concluded that the cleansing of the sanctuary meant the return of Christ when He would judge the world and the church cleansing them of sin. He calculated that the end of the 2300 days/years prophecy would come sometime during 1843 or 1844. Finally the Millerites settled on a date in October, 1844.

When Jesus did not arrive, of course disappointment and discouragement overtook the Millerite believers. Their error did not lie in the time prophecy but in their understanding of what the reference to the sanctuary meant. A number of Adventists realized that neither the earth nor the church was the sanctuary referred to. Biblical evidence simply did not support that conclusion. But they did find many passages about the heavenly sanctuary, where Christ ministers as High Priest. The only earthly sanctuary mentioned in the Bible was the tabernacle of Moses (Exodus 25:8), which the Jews had replaced with the Jerusalem Temple. But the Temple itself lay in ruins at the time Daniel penned his prophecy.

---

[1] LeRoy Froom, *Movement of Destiny* (Washington, D. C: Review and Herald Publishing Association, 1971), p. 55.

The letter to the Hebrews clearly indicates the existence of the heavenly sanctuary (Hebrews 6:19-20; 8:1-2; 9:11-12, 23-28). The same passages reveal that Christ now serves there as High Priest before the Father's throne. Because of His ministry there we can have confidence to approach God in faith, to draw near to Him in complete assurance of His love and forgiveness (Hebrews 10:19-22). The conclusion was obvious. The great event prophesied by Daniel is taking place in the heavenly sanctuary.

Christ ministers to us by His Holy Spirit from the heavenly sanctuary and metes out the benefits of His atonement on Calvary. His ministry in heaven falls into two parts, paralleling the activity of the high priest in the Hebrew tabernacle following the exodus from Egypt. In the tabernacle the priests made daily sacrifices for sin and by means of the blood of the offering the sins were transferred to the tabernacle's sanctuary. Once a year, on the Day of Atonement, the tabernacle sanctuary was cleansed of the accumulated sins of the people. In the same manner, Christ cleanses the heavenly sanctuary by the removal of the sins recorded there. That there exists such a heavenly record the Bible clearly teaches (Isa. 65:6 65:6; Jer. 17:1; Dan. 7:10; Mal. 3:16; Luke 10:20; Rev. 20:12).

Daniel 7 presents a panorama of world events until God's people reign with Him. It pictures the work of judgment conducted by the heavenly court before the throne of God when the record books are opened. Revelation 4 to 7 seem to parallel the judgment scene of Daniel 7. Both accounts indicate that God alone decides the eternal destiny of individuals. Revelation 14:7, which says, "fear God and give him glory, for the hour of his judgment has come," is highly significant in its account of the sequence of events related to the end of human history. It indicates that the hour of judgment precedes the sending forth of a warning message and the call for God's people to come out of apostate Christianity to take their stand on the commandments of God and the faith of Jesus Christ.[2] It reveals that we are now in the time of the pre-Advent judgment when the heavenly court sits in session in the presence of God the Father and Christ the High Priest.

-----

[2] See the context of the seventh verse in the entire chapter.

If we are now in the time of the pre-Advent judgment, when the heavenly record is being examined to see who is in Christ or not in Christ, obviously that examination had a beginning. In God's plan and operation every event has its moment in time. God does not limit Himself to arbitrary dates, and often acts when situations require it. But, based on the Biblical data, we can date many divine events that have occurred in the past quite accurately. Sometimes God does set up a timetable to follow. Once again, based on the Biblical data, it is possible to establish when the heavenly court began its pre-Advent investigation.

Daniel 8:14 indicates that God's "fullness of time," in this case the deliberation of the divine court, would begin at the end of the twenty-three hundred days/years prophecy, which is the historical date 1844. Biblical data stresses that the time prophecy began with the decree by Artaxerxes in 457 B.C. to rebuild Jerusalem. That prophecy ends in 1844.[3] From that moment in God's eternal plan the pre-Advent judgment has been taking place in heaven. When the verdict is finally in, the closing events of human history will swiftly begin. Christ the Saviour will descend in triumph to rescue His people, and as Lord execute the decision of the court. His people need not fear the pre-Advent judgment as it is on their behalf. When the names of the faithful come before the heavenly tribunal, Christ the High Priest pleads and intercedes for each one.

Revelation 14:6-12 indicates that during the period of the pre-Advent judgment, and just prior to the Lord's return, a specific gospel message will be proclaimed to all the world. An important aspect of that message is salvation through Christ alone. Included also is a summons to worship God as Creator in the face of increasing acceptance of evolution by many denominations and theologians. In addition, God's final message warns of a growing apostasy and the judgment that will overtake all who persist in allegiance to the apostate religious system.

Those who respond to the plea to worship the Creator will recognize that the seventh-day Sabbath is a sign of allegiance to Him, and Him alone. Observance of the Sabbath is also a part of the allegiance of those who "keep

_____

[3] Changing from B.C. to A.D. dates, we must allow for a one-year difference.

the commandments of God and the faith of Jesus." (Revelation 14:12)

The Holy Spirit will use the proclamation of the pre-Advent gospel to prepare the world and the church for judgment. This proclamation will occur while the heavenly tribunal sits, and constitutes God's final appeal to mankind.

The Seventh-day Adventist Church is the institutional instrument appointed by God to proclaim His last gospel message. Its thrust under divine mandate is two-pronged: (1) To preach Christ as the only Saviour to unbelieving people so as to bring them to salvation, and (2) To warn the churches of the coming judgment on apostasy while calling God's faithful people out of that apostasy. It is this calling-out aspect of the mission of the Seventh-day Adventist Church that is the most offensive to other denominations, since they see no need for it.

However much the idea is ridiculed and despised it cannot be stopped because it is based on Scripture and is from God. The time has come for its proclamation. We must beware that we do not reject the very thing God has established to accomplish His purpose and bring His people to final victory. He has entrusted the Seventh-day Adventist Church with a specific calling-out message. In His mercy He is providing His people the world over with a spiritual refuge as they become alert to the creeping apostasy taking over in many churches.

It is because God loves the world and His people that He is sending out, through the ministry of the Seventh-day Adventist Church, the message of Revelation 14:6-12. It is a message that **must** be preached and heard.

It did not take long for me to recognize that the Seventh-day Adventist Church is a unique institution interested in the whole person; that it is not a second-rate sect, but a dynamic and powerful spiritual movement. Utilizing the most sophisticated evangelistic techniques, it has set out to win the world for Christ. The great emphasis on His imminent return has not, as some would assume, caused unconcern about the condition of life in the world. On the contrary, the millions of dollars of tithe given by Adventists, as well as their generous offerings, support a fantastic and rapidly growing medical/evangelistic outreach into all parts of the world. Adventist missionaries are active in many countries where other denominations have closed down, preaching not only the Good News of salvation in

Christ but the Good Life in anticipation of the Lord's soon return.

Satan and all his powers of evil are marshaled against God's final message to the world. He has effectively dropped a veil across people's eyes so that they fail to recognize Biblical truth. By means of prejudice and misunderstanding Satan has cleverly kept people from hearing and heeding what the Adventist Church really teaches and represents.

Over the years critics have written many books and pamphlets against the Seventh-day Adventist Church. I myself have used anti-Adventist tracts in my past ministry. But now, after several years of intense and continuous study and evaluation, I know such works do not represent a complete understanding of the church's teachings and mission. Hence, they come to erroneous conclusions.

In spite of the trauma of my confrontation with the message of Adventism, I am thankful for what God did in bringing that confrontation about. In the process He fulfilled His promise and gave me a future and a hope. His plans for me are good, not evil. I rejoice daily that He led me into the Seventh-day Adventist Church, for it is just now reaching its maturity. Although its growth has been phenomenal, especially in the mission fields, its greatest hour lies just ahead. I am thrilled to be a part of it.

It is my conviction that every sincere Christian who loves the Lord and His Word, and who desires above all else to be found faithful and obedient, will, upon study and investigation of the gospel as taught by the Seventh-day Adventist Church, take a stand in favor of it. There is no other choice. Truth is truth. Although such a person may struggle with love for a congregation and denomination, it will finally be seen that such love can best be expressed by following God all the way, beckoning and encouraging others to do likewise.

The appearance of the Seventh-day Adventist Church on the stage of Christian history itself is a sign of Christ's soon coming. Signs are meant to be heeded and followed. It is a good sign, for it points to Jesus Christ, announces His soon return, and gathers His people to meet Him.

13

NEW BEGINNINGS

Much has happened in my life since that fateful Saturday in the late summer of 1968. Admittedly, the way was not easy. But I learned through the years that it is only in full surrender to Christ and His Lordship that one can find peace and security. It is only in praying, "Nevertheless, not my will, but thine be done," that one finds the path He has determined for one's life. Our Lord has a will for every person. That will can be known, and by His gracious help followed and obeyed.

REACTIONS

People have judged my decision to leave the Lutheran Church and unite with the Seventh-day Adventist Church in various ways. My closest friends, those who know me best and continue to maintain our relationship, have accepted my decision. Some of them do not agree with the rationale for that decision, and they have a right to disagree, but they continue to respect and honor my Christian convictions. Many of them have been far kinder to me than I was to Shirley at the time of her decision.

A few friends and former parishioners continued to trust me enough to listen to my witness concerning the truth about Seventh-day Adventism and its Christ-centeredness. They listened to the point where they, too, had their eyes opened by the Holy Spirit, are now keeping the seventh-day Sabbath and preparing for Christ's return. It was like throwing a rock into a pool and watching the ripple spread out in all directions.[1]

Others view my decision, and the witness it represents, quite differently. Some feel that it reveals a complete loss of sound judgment, that I was brain-washed. Some consider it the decision of an opportunist. Others believe I was forced to make it because my wife had done so. Several even judge it to be a cowardly act used to escape a difficult and trying situation. A few insist that it was only an **academic** decision and really doesn't have much significance in terms of faith.

Such attempts to interpret my decision represent a need, on the part of honest and sincere individuals, to find an explanation other than that of a search for truth. In view of the fact that, when Shirley made her initial decision, I preferred to judge her ill rather than consider that she might have encountered greater truth, I can understand such an attitude. At the time, Shirley's decision threatened many of my beliefs and convictions, leaving me feeling insecure. Eventually I realized that if what the Adventist Church teaches makes me feel that way, it may not be because something is wrong with what it teaches but with what I believed to be right. I'm certain that my decision has caused many people to feel as threatened and as insecure as I did. To them I am happy to say that they have no need to fear the truth.

Unless we are just interested in information, we must draw conclusions from what we have learned. We must take a stand. We must put truth into action. Such truth may challenge our presuppositions, and the foundations of our beliefs may tremble and threaten to collapse. Thus, rather than push on to truth, we may abandon the search for the sake of self-protection and begin to construct an elaborate defense system. We gather stratagems and ideas that support our presuppositions rather than those which challenge them. Frantically we defend what we have always believed and growth and learning cease.

I feel deeply for those searching, as I did, for a way of avoiding a confrontation with the Biblical truths espoused by

---

[1] The first edition of this book, which sold over 30,000 copies, was instrumental in the process by which a number of people elected to become part of the Advent movement.

the Seventh-day Adventist Church. But Christian love compels me to continue to bear witness to that which I know God wants them to see also.

As far as readers of this book are concerned, I rest my case in their hands as to whether or not God has truly been leading and guiding in my life. On the basis of the evidence I have presented here, they will have to make their own judgment. As for me: "I am not ashamed, for I know whom I have believed and I am sure that he is able to guard until that Day what has been entrusted to me." (2 Timothy 1:12)

LOVE FOR TRUTH

In the closing days of human history, truth is of supreme importance. Truth is more important than love. Love is always in the service of truth, truth is never at the mercy of love. Truth must take precedence over all human loyalties and affections. Crucial times demand crucial decisions. We must yearn for truth and diligently search it out. The psalmist prayed:

Lead me in thy truth, and teach me, for thou art the God of my salvation; for thee I wait all the day long. (Psalm 25:5)

Oh send out thy light and the truth; let them lead me, let them bring me to thy holy hill and to thy dwelling. (Psalm 43:3)

The psalmist also recognized that it was God's will that he learn and know eternal truth: "Behold, thou desirest truth in the inward being; therefore teach me wisdom in my secret heart." (Psalm 51:6) The prophet Isaiah spoke of a time when people have no desire for truth: "For truth has fallen in the public squares, and uprightness cannot enter. Truth is lacking, and he who departs from evil makes himself a prey." (Isaiah 59:14-15)

The Bible declares that Jesus Christ is the truth: "And the word became flesh and dwelt among us, full of grace and truth." (John 1:14) Furthermore, man was made to worship God and must do so as truthfully as possible: "God is spirit, and those who worship him must worship in spirit and truth." (John 4:24) Our worship of God is enhanced and deepened the more we know and apply His truth in our lives.

111

Christ and truth are synonymous. He said: "I am the way, and the truth, and the life; no one comes to the Father, but by me." (John 14:6) We must not only know and love truth, we must also obey and follow it. To do so will bring us greater enlightenment. Jesus said:

If you love me, you will keep my commandments. And I will pray to the Father, and he will give you another Counselor, to be with you for ever, even the Spirit of truth, whom the world cannot receive, because it neither sees him nor knows him; you know him, for he dwells with you, and will be in you. (John 14:15-17)

The Holy Spirit reveals His presence in our lives by the tangible results He produces in us and not by our feelings, or by some ecstatic experience. The spiritual gifts are not the highest attainment in the Christian experience. Full and complete obedience to truth is. Even those who have received a spiritual gift can have a more complete surrender to the Holy Spirit through the acceptance of all His truth. The primary evidence of being baptized, filled, with the Holy Spirit is love for Christ and love for His truth. One who is faithful is one who has faith in Christ and, by the power of the Spirit, obeys every command of God.

In behalf of His people Christ prayed to the Father that He would "sanctify them in the truth; thy word is truth." (John 17:17) Such a prayer harmonized with what He saw as His primary mission in the world: "For this I was born, and for this I have come into the world, to bear witness to the truth. Every one who is of the truth hears my voice." (John 18:37)

Paul underscores the centrality of truth in his admonition to all who turn away from knowledge of God:

Therefore, God gave them up in the lusts of their hearts to impurity, to the dishonoring of their bodies among themselves, because they exchanged the truth about God for a lie and worshipped the creature rather than the Creator, who is blessed forever! (Romans 1:24-25)[2]

Lust of the heart is simply going one's own way in the face of clear truth. To reject truth is a serious matter, and to refuse to search it out is dangerous.

Truth is the only defense against Satan: "Stand therefore, having girded your loins with truth." (Ephesians 6:14) Furthermore, Paul strongly counsels us to "guard the truth that has been entrusted to you by the Holy Spirit who dwells within us." (2 Timothy 1:14) This does not mean a denominational position, but the truth of the whole Bible. It does not mean the Christian tradition handed down to us by parents and grandparents, unless it is totally Scriptural.

God portrayed the seriousness with which He views truth and our relationship to it, when He warned:

> *For if we sin deliberately after receiving the knowledge of the truth, there no longer remains a sacrifice for sins, but a fearful prospect of judgment, and a fury of fire which will consume the adversaries. (Hebrews 10:26-27)*

For the Christian to deliberately turn away from truth, once it is known, is to turn away from Christ!

Obedience to truth involves the purification of life: "Having purified your souls by your obedience to the truth for a sincere love of the brethren, love one another earnestly from the heart." (1 Peter 1:22) We express love for each other and for our fellowmen when we witness to God's truth and follow it in practice. He desires to use His faithful people to demonstrate His expectations before the world by belief and practice. True love does not compromise the revealed will of God for sentimental reasons, or any other reasons. To compromise His will does not represent sacrificial love for the world, only compromise. True love, patterned after Christ's love, is ready and willing to suffer for the sake of truth.

---

[2] The truth of which Paul speaks in this passage is God's expectation that His people live holy and righteous lives. It is in that connection that he condemns homosexuality.

113

God wants us to make His truth known to all mankind. He also continues to call His faithful people's attention to the truth they have accepted and practiced, for the purpose of reinforcing their surrender and assuring them of His constant care: "Therefore I intend always to remind you of these things, though you know them and are established in the truth that you have." (2 Peter 1:12) We should demonstrate the same kind of concern as we relate in love to our fellow Christians. The apostle Peter said:

> *I think it right, as long as I am in this body, to arouse you by way of reminder, since I know that the putting off of my body will be soon, as our Lord Jesus Christ showed me. And I will see to it that after my departure you may be able at any time to recall these things. (2 Peter 1:13-15)*

One may **know** truth with the mind and intellect, but truth is not **inward** until, or unless, it has so captivated the individual that by the Spirit's power the necessary changes to bring life into harmony with it are made. "And by this we may be sure that we know him, if we keep his commandments. He who says, 'I know him' but disobeys his commandments is a liar, and the truth is not in him." (1 John 2:3-4) But being in possession of God's truth and being possessed by God's truth are not the same thing. If one only possesses the truth, it can be keep at a distance. But to be possessed by truth means coming under its dominion and control. As Jesus Christ is truth, He totally possesses and dwells in those who have surrendered by faith to Him. Here is the secret of spiritual power and victory: "The word of God abides in you, and you have overcome the evil one." (1 John 2:14)

NEW BEGINNING

Christ helps those begin their lives over again who seek truth and desire to live obediently under their heavenly Father's loving care. However, if they then sin, they have an Advocate with the Father, Jesus Christ the totally righteous One. Wearing the cloak of His righteousness, they stand before the Father, and because of Jesus and His love, God forgives.

114

The sinner who repents and surrenders to God by faith in Christ finds a whole new life, a new experience. The Christian believer who has walked with the Lord for many years also experiences a new beginning each day, for God's grace is renewed every day. In forgiveness and peace each new day can be faced with renewed grace, renewed power from God. If the believer fails and falls, God picks the fallen up and sends him on the way again. Every day with Him is a new beginning. God's will and plan for every life is full of new beginnings. That's what makes the Christian life so thrilling and exciting! It is certainly not boring.

God has proven His trustworthiness and faithfulness to His people over and over again. The believer can be confident that God will never forsake His people, never leave them, never lead them up a dead end. Our God is a God of redemption. He redeems the situations and circumstances of life and turns them into blessings.

In fulfilling His promise to give me a future and a hope, He gave me a new beginning built on past experiences with Him. He did not forsake me. It is still His will that I serve Him in the Christian ministry. Now, however, in the context of the Seventh-day Adventist Church and its mission. I know, and am assured, that as I obey and follow Him, He will continue to watch over me and my family. I have His assurance that He will use me in the work of His kingdom in a way and in a place where I can be the most effective and make the greatest contribution.

Grateful for the past, for the spiritual heritage that is mine, and looking to the future, I await the unfolding of my Lord's will. I followed truth, and in the process God granted me a new beginning. I am excited about the message and mission of the Seventh-day Adventist Church! I am excited about the future!

14

CONFIRMATION

The story you have read so far covers the period between the Fateful Saturday in 1968 and April 24, 1971 when I was baptized into the Seventh-day Adventist Church. What has happened since? How has God been leading in our lives since Shirley lifted her hands in praise during the Service at Pioneer Memorial Church when I joined her as a Seventh-day Adventist? Both of us feel that subsequent events have served as divine confirmation of the decisions we made after much struggle and pain. Confirmation of the promise He made to me in Jeremiah 29:11, to give me "a future and a hope."

GOD'S LOVING DISCIPLINE

Ministry was certainly not over for me! Ministry was just beginning in ways I could never have thought possible! Ellen G. White wrote:

God brings His people near Him by close, testing trials, by showing them their own weakness and inability, and by teaching them to lean upon Him as their only help and safeguard. Then His object is accomplished. They are prepared to be used in every emergency, to fill important positions of trust, and to accomplish the grand purposes for which their powers were given them. God takes men upon trial; He proves them on the right hand and on the left, and thus they are educated, trained, disciplined.[1]

There is profound wisdom in the above statement. Wisdom at the very center of which is the cross of Jesus Christ. Wisdom given by God to Ellen White in the crucible of her own suffering as a disciple of Christ. To follow Christ is to walk the way He walked, and He walked the way of the cross. To follow Christ is to bear the cross. It is the way of submission, of discipline. Every Christian has a cross to carry. The nature of my cross, your cross, will be revealed as we follow Christ.

God, our Father, treats us like legitimate children and does not hesitate to exercise divine discipline in order to prepare us for the work He has for us to do, for the life He wants us to live. Why? So that "we may share in his holiness." His loving discipline, which is not always pleasant to experience, will always "produce a harvest of righteousness and peace for those who have been trained by it." (Hebrews 12:10-11 NIV)

The God with whom we have to do is not a doting old grandfather. He is the Majesty in the heavens. He has a will for us and makes it known. The choice is ours concerning whether we will obey His will or not. And there are consequences to our choice. He graciously gives the future and the hope He promises but not apart from the receiver's surrender and acceptance of whatever that future might hold.

He redeems us **from** sin and **for** righteousness and service. He exercises His sanctifying power in the life of the redeemed so as to make them fit instruments for His purposes and His service. The believer does not live for himself alone. He lives for God. Paul said: "to me to live is Christ." (Philippians 1:21 NIV) Such surrender was not meant just for Paul. We cannot say that such was only his religious experience and that ours may be different. His words are the Word of God. Such surrender to grace and discipline and discipleship is expected from every true believer.

God shows the way, gives the promise, and then waits for our response. Only He knows the end from the beginning. We must walk **by** faith and **in** faith. God made His

---

[1] *Testimonies*, Vol. 4, p. 86.

promise to me; human beings made none. No influential person in the Adventist Church gave me any assurance concerning future service. No enticing bait was dangled before my eyes. Had it been I would have suspected falsehood and deception. I had no idea what would happen to me when I decided to join the Seventh-day Adventist Church. For all I knew I might have to find other employment and take my place in the church as a layman. But I did not believe that God called me to ministry, after seven years of training, for only ten years of service.

MASTER OF THEOLOGY

Shortly after my baptism the Seventh-day Adventist Church informed me that the church would sponsor me financially for the remainder of my studies at Andrews University. The course work for the Master of Theology degree was completed by the end of the fall quarter 1971. My thesis, "Preaching The Gospel of The Parousia" (second advent), was completed in time for graduation in June 1972. Rather large for a master's thesis, 371 pages plus bibliography, the writing of it gave me the opportunity to survey both the Old and New Testament teaching concerning last day events and the return of Christ. Especially in relation to the preaching of His return.

It helped me to see the reasons for the existence of the Seventh-day Adventist Church and its evangelistic ministry in the entire world. Three conclusions became apparent: 1)-We have been called to preach a historic Gospel concerning the literal and personal return of Christ. 2)-Contemporary people need a reintroduction to the spiritual heritage they have abandoned, as it is the only message that can resolve their dilemmas and relieve their anxiety. 3)-The Gospel of Christ's return has been designed by God to meet the needs of contemporary people who are experiencing the specific anxieties of *kairos* (crisis) time. Acknowledgments include:

> *to my wife, Shirley, who bore the brunt of the reactions of a deeply perplexed man, I owe a debt of gratitude I can never pay. She can only cancel it out as love bears all things, believes all things, and hopes all things.*

119

Meanwhile the Michigan Conference of the SDA Church invited me to be associate pastor of the Tabernacle Church in Battle Creek, Michigan where we moved in January 1972. Two major things took place during the year we lived in Battle Creek. I was able to make the transition to the Adventist approach to ministry, and complete the major part of writing the first edition of this book, published in 1974.

In January 1973 the Michigan Conference appointed me pastor of the Fairplain Seventh-day Adventist Church near Benton Harbor, Michigan. I had requested permission to enter the Doctor of Ministry program at Andrews University and was moved to Fairplain so that I could do so on a quarter on, quarter off, basis. That is to say, I was allowed to take courses every other quarter.

On January 27, 1973, the Seventh-day Adventist Church recognized and reaffirmed my ordination to the gospel ministry in a special service in Pioneer Memorial Church at Andrews University. Led by the President of the General Conference, Elder Robert Pierson, I was set apart for the Adventist ministry by the laying on of hands.

DOCTOR OF MINISTRY

In addition to my ministry as pastor of the Fairplain Church, two other significant events occurred. The Doctor of Ministry degree was conferred upon me in June 1975, on the basis of a Project Report entitled: "A Dialogical Evaluation of A Series of Eight Sermons Preached in the Benton Harbor Church of Seventh-day Adventists From April 6 to June 1, 1974." The study was designed to find the answers to two basic questions: 1)-Was my preaching practice consistent with my theology of preaching? 2)-Would the training of members in listening skills increase their ability to recall sermonic data thus contributing to Christian growth and attitudinal change?

Secondly, the results of the doctoral study were published in book form by *Review and Herald Publishing Association*, in 1978. Under the title *It's A Two Way Street*, the book constituted a Seventh-day Adventist theology of preaching.[2]

What is the significance of the above in relation to God's promise concerning my future in ministry? I relate these events only to demonstrate how God was leading in a new direction. Once again I followed His lead as doors opened for further education and preparation. During the years 1972-1975 there developed within me the growing conviction that God was preparing me for a teaching ministry. I had always been happy in parish work, and had no other goals than to serve as preacher and pastor. Except that the Lord was laying another goal upon my heart. Confirmation of that goal was academic success in two graduate programs, plus the publication of two books and a number of articles in church papers such as *These Times, Advent Review, The Ministry, Signs of The Times.* Further confirmation came when, during the spring quarter of 1977, the SDA Theological Seminary at Andrews University invited me to teach one section of preaching.

TO THE PHILIPPINES

The point was reached in my spiritual pilgrimage when I knew that God was preparing me for a new direction in ministry. Just exactly how that new direction would be revealed, I had no idea. But I was waiting in almost breathless expectancy to see what He would do next. His plan, His future, my hope, was continuing to unfold. How it unfolded! Already abundantly blessed with confirmation of having made the right decision in becoming a Seventh-day Adventist, the next events were startling.

It began innocently enough. With a phone call from a Field Secretary of the General Conference of Seventh-day Adventists, and then a visit to our home on a warm Monday evening in May, 1978. Four months later we were in the Philippines! He came on behalf of the church with a call to serve on the Faculty of the SDA Theological Seminary, Far East, which was being located on a new campus about 35

---

[2] Out of print by 1986, the book was republished, in an enlarged edition, by Andrews University Press in 1987 under the title *The Last Word.*

miles south of Manila in Cavite province. The need was so urgent an answer was required within a week!

The next four months were hectic. My ministry at Fairplain was brought to a close. We attended the Mission Institute, orientation for all new missionaries prior to departure, at Andrews University. Had a large garage sale. Packed the household goods we would be taking with us. Put our house up for sale. Visited all our relatives, and took off for the Far East stopping enroute at Los Angeles, Hawaii, and Guam.

We arrived in Manila early one morning on a Philippine Airlines DC-10. Beneath us was our first sight of rice paddies, banana plants, coconut groves, nipa huts, and swarms of people with tawny skin and beautiful black eyes and hair. The heat and humidity enveloped us like a suffocating blanket. But we had arrived and our great adventure began!

Fully expecting to remain for at least six years, and possibly more, our term of service turned out to be approximately three years. During that time we shared in the development of a new seminary curriculum, as well as the design and construction of faculty homes, the seminary building and library, and student housing. I taught courses in preaching, worship, leadership, pastoral care, and theology. My students came from the Philippines, Indonesia, Japan, Korea, Taiwan, Singapore, Malaysia, Solomon Islands, Africa, and even from Finland. What a mix! What a challenge!

Our children were off to Far Eastern Academy in Singapore. Twelve hundred miles away! We saw them only at Christmas and for the "summers." It was difficult for them to adjust to life in Singapore and at the Academy, so it was for family reasons that our tour of missionary service ended after only three years. When we returned to the U.S.A., I felt that my work in the Philippines was not yet finished. Still I believed that the entire experience was part of God's will for me, that I was still in His training school. I felt a little bit like I felt when at 25 years of age my father said to me: "I've taught you everything I know and you still don't know anything."

Much comfort was derived from the kind letter we received from Dr. Leslie Hardinge, Dean of the Seminary in the Far East, in which he said:

May I express my regrets that circumstances beyond your control have compelled you to cut short your stay here. You were left with the only option possible, and you and Shirley have decided to take it. I am confident that the good Lord, who brought your family here, has a part in this decision, and is working out the pathway along which He purposes you to walk. When you get together in the States as a family, I am sure you will be able to see the grand design more carefully.

Yes, God was still fulfilling His promise concerning the future. But for awhile it was difficult to understand just how He was going about it. But before I tell you that part of the story let me share some of the impact service in the Philippines made upon my life. In retrospect there is absolutely no doubt in my mind that it was God's will that we go to the Far East, and also that we return after just three years.

The first impact was in terms of learning. I learned to appreciate special values found in Filipino culture. Such as the way in which the person is supported. There is great personal interdependence in which every effort is made to avoid confrontation, embarrassment, and exploitation of vulnerability. Any lengths are sought to avoid crisis because it would disrupt smooth relationships.

Filipino's see life wholistically. Because of this, there seemed to be an absence of the logical thought so valued in the west. Euphemisms were used extensively to talk around a subject instead of speaking directly and risking strain on a valued relationship. Filipinos are not particularistic, not given to detail, and usually do not think in lineal sequence. Translated into daily life this fact means that in heavy city traffic it is not important to stay in a rigid traffic pattern determined by lines on the pavement. Such lines are easily crossed because what is seen is the flow of traffic rather than the need to stay within boundaries.

One must learn to see the flow of traffic, and become a part of it, or he will not survive. Perhaps I learned to see it too well, for within weeks of our return to the U.S.A., I was involved in the first major car accident in my life. All because I was no longer paying close attention to the lines on the pavement. What I did learn was that people do not always see obvious things in the same way.

The second impact was in terms of writing. The whole experience made such an indelible impression upon me that I wrote another book. A book with a strange title: *Boiled Rice and Gluten.*[3] It is not a cookbook, but a different kind of book about missionary service.   It tells it like it **was**. Started in the Philippines as a therapeutic exercise, the book was finished in late 1985.

Also started in the Philippines was a book entitled *Sing A New Song!*[4] Based on the lecture notes I had prepared for my courses in worship, it is a discussion of what I feel is the need for worship renewal among Adventists today.

Why do I tell you about these books? Because they too confirm God's leading in my decision to join the Seventh-day Adventist Church. They too are part of the fulfillment of His promise to give me a future and a hope. They are a very important part of the new direction in ministry which He has opened to me. If anyone had suggested, twenty years ago, that I would author books I think I would have laughed hilariously. Nothing was further from my mind. One doesn't simply decide to write a book. The author must be given a burden. He must be given a message. The books in my library that I value the most highly, have been born out of pain.   Besides, writing is lonely work.   Especially if the writer is not a loner.   I have discovered that it takes a great deal of discipline to write a book.

RETURN

Our return to the U.S.A., while welcome in some ways in that we came back to a familiar culture, was also sad. Because I felt it to be a regression. Once again I could not understand just how God was working. No teaching positions were available, instead the Michigan Conference appointed me pastor at Grand Haven and Wright. I went reluctantly. Why would God prepare me for a teaching ministry and then not let me teach?   Only one reason.   There must have been something He still wanted to teach me before He would let me teach others.

Even though I accepted the call reluctantly, the year we spent in Grand Haven and Wright was the best pastoral experience I have ever had! It was good for me, and it was good for Shirley. The members of those two congregations

---

[3] Berrien Springs, Mich., POINTER Publications, 1986.

[4] Berrien Springs, Mich., Andrews University Press, 1984.

just loved us to pieces, and we loved them, and it was such a healing experience. One that we needed so badly. It was truly a Sabbath year for us, a time of rest, of refreshment, the healing of wounds and of soul after a decade of intense doctrinal and spiritual struggle.

In June 1982 I was called to the Seventh-day Adventist Theological Seminary at Andrews University to serve as Director of Seminary Student Life, Director of the Doctor of Ministry program, and professor of worship and preaching. I love my work! I love Andrews University. It is like walking on holy ground each time I set foot on the campus. I love to get up each morning and go to work. I love to come home at the end of each day knowing that I am doing what God wants me to do, what He has prepared me to do. In fact, I am convinced that my entire life has been the preparation, under His direction, for the work I am doing now. Confirmation, once again, in being granted the privilege of responsible service, of the decision to become a member of the Seventh-day Adventist Church. God has been unfailing in fulfilling His promise to give me a future and a hope! To Him be all the glory and honor!

OUR HOME

When we came back to Berrien Springs in the summer of 1982 it was to move into the home we designed together and built in 1973. Confirmation again, we believe, of God's providential will and protection. I cannot close this chapter without telling you the story of our home. Until 1973 we did not enjoy the privilege of owning our own home. We lived in parsonages during the Lutheran phase of our lives, both of them very old and in need of repair. I recall that in our first parsonage there was only two electrical circuits and in the winter every time the furnace would go on the lights would dim down.

In Battle Creek we lived in a parsonage, though a much newer one than we had enjoyed up to that time. However, when we came to the Fairplain Church there was no parsonage and we were faced with either renting or building. At first we rented an old, drafty, farm house but would have preferred our own home. But that was not possible. As a Lutheran minister I earned $400.00 a month in 1961 and $600.00 a month by 1970. It was not possible for me to save. With no savings, no property, how could I possibly think of building a house?

Meanwhile Dr. Bigford was invited to join the medical staff at Andrews University. The Bigford's bought a house with considerable acreage near Berrien Springs, and they asked us if we would consider building next to them if they gave us some land. What were we to say? Once again the Lord used their Christian hospitality and generosity to make possible the impossible. It was an answer to prayer. But the decision was contingent upon the answer to two questions: 1)-Could we get a mortgage with no equity of our own? and 2)-Would the health department approve the soil for septic drainage.

We can still recall the day the soil was tested and how we four prayed together, holding hands in a circle in the middle of the field. The permit was granted! With the property as equity the mortgage was granted!

In order to build our house within the limits of the mortgage we had to design it and do the work ourselves. So while pastoring the Fairplain Church, and beginning the course work for my doctorate, we began to build. Ground was broken in May and we moved into our own home in November. Every spare moment for nine months, many evenings, every Sunday, my vacation, was devoted to construction. The house, including landscaping, was completed exactly within the budget to the penny!

It was painful to put it up for sale when we went to the Philippines. But it didn't sell. Many people looked at it and liked it. A retired couple made a downpayment, parked their travel trailer in the yard preparatory to moving in, and then mysteriously changed their minds. With no buyer it had to be rented for the entire three years we were overseas. When we returned we lived in it for only two months before moving to Grand Haven and renting it out again.

Why all the uncertainty about our beloved home? Confirmation again! It was here waiting for us when I was called to Andrews University. We have been enjoying it again for the past five years and I am writing these words seated in my study, looking out on the very spot where we held the prayer meeting about the building permit back in 1973.

People have asked me if I regret my decision to become a Seventh-day Adventist Christian. If the story you have been reading was yours, how would you answer that question? Everything that has taken place in our lives since that decision is handwriting on the wall as far as I am concerned. God's promise is as true for you as it is for me, or for anyone else: "We know that in everything God works for good with those who love him, who are called according to his purpose." (Romans 8:28)

God has blessed so abundantly. He has more than fulfilled His promise. I have a future in the Seventh-day Adventist Church and its ministry. I have hope in the soon return of the Savior. The question now is: What will He have me do for Him now, for the future is really His not mine.

15

AFFIRMATION

For ten years I was a Lutheran minister. For the past sixteen years I have been a Seventh-day Adventist minister. What I say in this chapter is based on a view from the inside of the Adventist Church.

No doubt you would be curious, were we speaking face to face, and ask me if I still feel the same way about the SDA Church after sixteen years. The answer is yes, yes I do. However, my initial excitement at having found a Bible-believing church has been sobered by the challenges that constantly face any dedicated Christian witness. The SDA Church lives and works in the same world together with all other churches. It is faced with the same challenges, the same temptations, that others face.

Having said that, however, let me also say that I believe the Seventh-day Adventist Church possesses the kind of spiritual resources that will see it through triumphant until Jesus comes. Those resources are primarily threefold: 1)-The written Word of God, 2)-The guidance and counsel found in the writings of Ellen G. White, referred to by Adventists as the Spirit of Prophecy, and 3)-Dedicated, born-again, believers who fervently believe in the message and mission of this church and support it faithfully, even sacrificially.

CONTEND FOR THE FAITH

The Seventh-day Adventist Church needs more people like that. People who will come and help spread the Gospel of the soon coming Savior as well as "contend for the faith which was once for all delivered to the saints." (Jude 3)

Any Christian who studies the Bible, who is sensitive to the spirit of the age, whose spiritual eyes are open, knows about this call of God to contend for the faith. To contend for Bible truth! To contend for historic Christianity! To contend for the validity of God's revelation in a most skeptical and humanistic time! He knows that God has made him a disciple for such a time as this! He counts it all joy for the privilege of suffering with Christ in the proclamation of the only truth that will save souls and get the world ready for the final events of history. This is no time to be silent. This is the time to stand up and be counted for Jesus Christ!

In 1857 Ellen White had a vision of what she called "The Shaking." She saw the people of God engaged in a great internal struggle. She described the scene in this way:

> *Evil angels crowded around them, pressing their darkness upon them, to shut out Jesus from their view, that their eyes might be drawn to the darkness that surrounded them, and they distrust God and next murmur against Him. Their only safety was in keeping their eyes directed upward.*[1]

She saw some of God's people who were indifferent and careless, who did not resist the darkness around them and were ultimately lost. Others earnestly prayed for divine assistance and were encouraged by the Lord.

> *I asked the meaning of the shaking I had seen, and was shown that it would be caused by the straight testimony called forth by the counsel of the True Witness to the Laodiceans. This will have an effect upon the heart of the receiver, and will lead him to exalt the standard and pour forth the straight truth. Some will not bear this straight testimony. They will rise up against it, and this will cause a shaking among God's people.*[2]

What will cause the shaking of the church? The straight testimony. I believe the straight testimony to be

---

[1] Ellen G. White, *Testimonies Vol. 1*, p.180.

[2] *Ibid*, p.181.

the unvarnished and unequivocal Word of God. That straight testimony will be called forth from the faithful by the True Witness who is Jesus Christ Himself, and it will be directed to the Laodiceans. That is to say, to the members of the last day church that is neither hot nor cold but lukewarm in faith and witness, and which has managed to keep Jesus on the outside where He stands and knocks. When the True Witness calls forth the straight testimony, and His faithful witnesses proclaim it, the shaking will come.

Sobering yet thrilling words! Sobering because God's people carry the responsibility of guarding the truth of God's Word in its purity and power. Thrilling because God will vindicate that responsibility. The faithful will be granted victory, while the unfaithful will be shaken out of the church. Why? Because, as the return of the Lord draws near, God will distinguish between true and false godliness.

> *The time is not far distant when the test will come to every soul. The mark of the beast will be urged upon us. Those who have step by step yielded to worldly demands and conformed to worldly customs will not find it a hard matter to yield to the powers that be, rather than subject themselves to derision, insult, threatened imprisonment, and death. The contest is between the commandments of God and the commandments of men. In this time the gold will be separated from the dross in the church. True godliness will be distinguished from the appearance and tinsel of it. Many a star that we have admired for its brilliancy will then go out in darkness. Chaff like a cloud will be borne away on the wind, even from places where we see only floors of rich wheat. All who assume the ornaments of the sanctuary, but are not clothed with Christ's righteousness, will appear in the shame of their own nakedness.*[3]

To whom do you think she is speaking? She is speaking to members of the Seventh-day Adventist Church first of all! I like that kind of talk! It has the Spirit of the Bible in it, the Spirit of God, the Spirit of the Truth. If you are a true disciple of Jesus you cannot help but recognize the

---

[3] Ellen G. White, *Testimonies*, Vol. 5, p.81.

sound of truth and the inspiration of the Lord. Doesn't it make you want to shout "hallelujah!?"

This is not the false teaching that the world and the church will get better and better before Jesus comes. This is the straight testimony that the opposite will actually be true. The world will certainly not get better, and its continuing precipitous slide into sin and all manner of perversion will have an effect on the life of the church. The lure of the world will entice the church. Faithful believers will engage in a fierce struggle to maintain the faith and contend for the faith. But there will be a remnant that will remain true to Christ and His principles, the Ten Commandments. That remnant will be sanctified in the Truth. Yet, it will have to remain vigilant so that while it is spending its time, money, and energy winning the world, the world will not win the Church.

I am glad to belong to a church that God loves so much that He does not hesitate to speak such a word. I heard so very little of such a word in years past. What I did hear of it was virtually lost as my former church began to merge and compromise belief in the process. My little voice was swallowed up in the ocean of liberalism, evolutionism, and humanism in which my church was sinking. But the Seventh-day Adventist Church is afloat and I am able to add my voice to its loud cry for righteousness and submission to the Word of God. That cry is directed first to its own constituency, and secondly to the rest of Christianity and the world.

Because of its consistent adherence to Scripture and its strong sense of community, the Seventh-day Adventist Church has been able to resist theological erosion up to the present time. But the challenge to continue such resistance with determination is ever present. It was once said that the price of liberty is eternal vigilance. The same is true when it comes to the integrity of the faith once delivered to the saints. Devout Adventists have known for a long time that whatever is given to the Gospel cause cannot be lost unless too little is given. They have known that they will conquer only if the pure Word of God is maintained no matter the cost. They have known that to compromise on one single point is to be in grave danger of losing all. Theirs has been a stubborn faith. Often criticized as being insular and legalistic. But, to paraphrase Scripture, what is to be gained by rubbing shoulders with the world and in the process yielding to the world's temptations?   Yes, it is a risky business to represent the Lord in this world. It cost Him His life!

The Seventh-day Adventist Church is committed to dealing responsibly with the Scriptures.   This commitment is essential or future generations of theologians and constituents will have no criteria by which they can solve doctrinal-moral problems.   God's call to His Church is not only to preach the Gospel to all nations but to "Guard, through the Holy Spirit who dwells in us, the treasure which has been entrusted to you." (2 Timothy 1:14 NAS) The treasure, of course, is the Word of God. The Church looks to its theologians for doctrinal guidance, for the protection of the faith. The Seventh-day Adventist Church has no intention of committing theological suicide by cutting itself off from the very source of its life and power, the Bible.   The whole of the Word of God is to be believed and obeyed by His people.

> *Christ declared, "As the Father gave me commandment, even so I do. If ye keep my commandments, ye shall abide in my love, even as I have kept my Father's commandments and abide in His love."   Let all who understand the abiding claims of the law of God, yield implicit obedience to every requirement given in the Word.   The convictions of the Holy Spirit are warnings which it is dangerous to disregard.   Christ declared that those who do His words are like a man who built his house upon a rock.   This house the tempest and flood could not sweep away.   Those who do not do Christ's words are like the man who built his house upon the sand.   Storm and tempest beat upon that house, and it fell, and great was the fall of it.   It was an entire wreck.   The result of professing to keep the law of God, yet walking contrary to the principles of that law, is seen in the wrecked house.   Those who make a profession while failing to obey cannot stand the storm of temptation.   One act of disobedience weakens the power to see the sinfulness of the second act.   One little disregard of "Thus saith the Lord" is sufficient to stop the promised blessing of the Holy Spirit.   By disobedience the light once so precious becomes obscure.[4]*

---

[4] Ellen G. White, *Manuscript #148*, (1899).

Mrs. White is speaking of disobedience to the written Word of God. The only way to be spared the consequences of which she speaks is to avoid their cause. The clear testimony, the straight testimony, of the Church can only be destroyed by means of a corruption in its interpretation of the Bible. Back in the Middle Ages Satan had his agents in the schools of the church, said Martin Luther, and through them caused the Scriptures to become

> *like a broken net and no one would be restrained by it,*
> *but everyone made a hole in it wherever it pleased him*
> *to poke his snout, and followed his own opinions,*
> *interpreting and twisting Scripture any way he pleased.*[5]

Together with Luther the Seventh-day Adventist Church has always believed that the Scriptures must be taken as simple and literal truth. To depart from the literal sense and meaning of the Bible is to undermine the very doctrines proclaimed by Scripture, and swings wide the theological door letting in all kinds of perversions of the Christian faith. All doctrines come from Scripture and any kind of uncertainty with respect to Biblical interpretation will eventually result in uncertainty concerning faith, morals, and ethics.

The Seventh-day Adventist Church is aware that much larger and influential churches have committed theological suicide by a contamination of Scriptural interpretation. It is convinced that the Bible is not a confusing document, but one that reveals a clear and unambiguous message from God to man. The Word of God is the greatest treasure of the church. To lose the Word of God would be to lose everything. To adopt the idea that the Bible is only the human response to God's activity, that it is only a production of the church's faith, is to lose the Bible as authoritative revelation. As a result doctrine is seen to be unimportant, and growing skepticism takes the place of faith.

---

[5] Martin Luther in *Word and Sacrament III*, ed. Robert H. Fischer, Vol. XXXVII in *Luther's Works*, American Edition, ed. Jaroslav Pelikan and Helmut T. Lehmann (Philadelphia: Fortress Press, 1961), pp. 13-14.

EVANGELICAL CRISIS

Most of the readers of this book will be members of the Seventh-day Adventist Church, or of some other evangelical church. There is no question that conservative evangelical churches are growing today, while more liberal churches are not. Which simply indicates that there is a very large group of people in American society who are hungry for, and searching for, Biblical truth and a firm, unshakable, faith. Conservative evangelical publishing houses are selling more books than ever before, and conservative journals such as *Christianity Today* have a wide circulation.

In spite of the above, evangelicals seem to be uncertain today about many theological/doctrinal issues. However, the most important issue evangelicals face today is the understanding of Biblical authority, or the way in which the Bible is interpreted. This issue is critical for evangelicals who have always confessed faith in the authority of the Bible as the revelation of God. All of evangelical thinking about life, about salvation, and about all other related matters, rests on acceptance of the Bible as the final arbitrator. This faith in the Word of God evangelicals hold in common. Seventh-day Adventists share that faith in the Scriptures.

In spite of this common confession there are many today who see the evangelical churches facing a grave crisis. Not a crisis of faith in the Bible as God's Word, but a crisis concerning how the Bible is to be interpreted. What does one do when the thinkers of the church, who confess faith in Biblical authority, reach contradictory conclusions relative to issues faced by the Church? Does the church read Scripture through culture, or culture through Scripture? Does truth, doctrine, arise out of the life of the congregation or out of Scripture? Is truth what a congregation confesses it to be, or is it derived from the Word of God? If truth is whatever a congregation confesses it to be then my wife and I could have remained in our former church. If truth is confessional, rather than revelational, then both Sabbath and Sunday keepers are following truth. But can that be so?

You and I will not be held accountable, in the final judgment, on the basis of what our congregation or denomination believes, but on the basis of whether or not our lives are in harmony with the Word of God. When one Bible book is pitted against another, when Paul is made to argue and dispute with Paul, then the individual believer must study each issue in relation to every Bible text that impinges upon it, pray earnestly for guidance from the Holy Spirit, and then act on the convictions arrived at. Always look for the harmony in the Word of God, not for what appears to be contradictions.

It should give you some comfort to know that you do not have to be an expert in Hebrew and Greek to understand the Bible or to arrive at accurate convictions. Remember, it is the Holy Spirit who is your Teacher and He will never lead you astray. One of the greatest events in human history was when the Bible was placed in the hands of ordinary and devout Christian believers, when it was no longer the private domain of theologians and scholars who were thought to possess esoteric knowledge. In my own pastoral experience I have made the acquaintance of persons who have evidenced deep spiritual wisdom and Bible knowledge with but limited education.

Radically divergent views on the part of evangelical thinkers can only result in the tragedy of polarization and pluralism. You may be faced with the need to find a church in which there is unity on essential theological issues, and where Biblical authority is still the foundation. You and I both know that once Biblical authority is abandoned there will follow a deterioration of faith and witness. Evangelism will go by the wayside, spiritual life will dry up, and apostasy will capture the church. Which is precisely why our Lord calls to us and says:

> *Fallen, fallen, is Babylon the great! . . Come out of her, my people, that you may not participate in her sins and that you may not receive of her plagues; for her sins have piled up as high as heaven, and God has remembered her iniquities. (Rev. 18:2-5 NAS)*

Martin Luther heard that call and separated from the Roman church; when you hear it you may be required, as I was, to separate from another church, and join a people who stand on the Word of God.

How one views the Bible is pivotal to his faith. What you see depends on where you stand. If your stand is skeptical you will doubt just about everything in the Book. If your stand is dialectical, you will see no harmony in the Bible only inconsistencies. You will have one Bible writer arguing with another. If your stand is dissatisfaction with what the Bible says on a particular issue, you will simply ignore the passages you do not like, which is what I did with the Sabbath texts for some time. If your stand is cultural, you will be able to cast aside many things in the Bible as culturally conditioned. If you see the Sabbath only as an expression of Jewish culture rather than as established at creation by God Himself, then you can readily cast it aside. If you are what is known as a progressive thinker, then you will be tempted to include current beliefs, though they be in contradiction to Scripture, as divine truth. You would see the Bible as historically limited and contemporary human wisdom progressive and more reliable.

But if your stand is *sola scriptura*, the Bible interpreting the Bible harmoniously, then you will see what so many thousands have seen before you. That it is God's Holy Word, absolutely reliable and trustworthy, to be believed and obeyed.

ELLEN G. WHITE

The reader will, no doubt, be very interested in my views concerning the role of Mrs. White in the Adventist faith since I wrote the tenth chapter of this book sixteen years ago. Especially in the light of attempts to discredit her during those intervening years.

Every church must develop an authentic form of spirituality, and it must be looked for within its own tradition. The spirituality of the Seventh-day Adventist Church must, therefore, be sought within its own tradition. That tradition rests first upon the Bible, and secondly upon the influence of Ellen G. White. She is perhaps the most important single factor, outside of Scripture, that has contributed to what others see as the strange, pervasive, and strong cohesion of the Seventh-day Adventist Church. In a most positive sense she is the spiritual godmother of the SDA Church.

The writings of Mrs. White are the critical link between Adventists and their past. As I said in chapter ten, her writings are a fence along the side of the road which would protect a very pluralistic Church from veering off the Biblical path in its search for an authentic spirituality. From the very beginning of Christianity there has been a constant battle with all the forces seeking to pervert the faith. One of the major purposes of Mrs. White's counsel is to illuminate, and give us confidence in, the earliest periods of

Christian history as revealed in Scripture, as well as inspire us with insight into major events that highlight victories in the search for that spirituality, such as the Reformation.

The counsel the SDA Church has received through Mrs. White, with its roots firmly planted in the revelation of God, is designed to help us live as Christians in a culture that was once Christian but is no longer. To be able to do so we must rely on the same resources that made it possible for the early Christians to live faithful lives in pagan cultures. While the apostolic church constituted the first generation of believers after Christ, we, today, are the first generation of believers after "Christendom." A small minority in a world, in a society, that is not in harmony with, but increasingly and aggressively hostile and antagonistic to, Biblical Christianity. The early Christians drew lines and made distinctions, many of which have become blurred or non-existent in modern times when good is called evil and evil good, and to which Mrs. White recalls our attention. So that we may live the Christian faith with clarity and nonambiguity in a most bewildering age.

In order to discover an authentic spirituality we must go back to the sources. Never have we had more to learn from the formative years of Christianity. Never have Adventists had more to learn from the formative years of their tradition. Those resources are the Bible and the writings of Ellen G. White. To avoid either of these would be to shortcircuit our search for a spirituality, and would present us with the danger of coming up with a spirituality that is not authentic. Today, because of the erosion of Biblical truth and deep commitment to it, we can learn more from those who stand in opposition to the modern and secular brand of Christianity.

Many writers have influenced my own search for a spirituality. Such as Martin Luther, Johan Arndt, Jacob Spener, O. H. Hallesby, a Norwegian pietist, C. O. Rosenious, a Swedish pietist, Paavo Ruotsalainen, a Finnish pietist, Dietrich Bonhoeffer, a German theologian and martyr, A. W. Tozer, a theologian of the Christian Alliance, and James Stewart. However, no writer has had such germinal influence upon my own developing spirituality than Ellen G. White. I am still processing the impact of her work on my life and faith. In my judgment, while her works contain reliable theology, their primary intent is spiritual. God has blessed the Seventh-day Adventist Church with this rich resource of spiritual direction for a three-fold purpose: 1)-To help individuals come to know Jesus Christ, 2)-To help them become Christlike, and 3)-To help them prepare for His second coming.

If the purpose of spiritual friendship is to affirm faith and commitment, to explore the nature of the faith relationship, to confront with respect to areas of life needing change in attitude and behavior, then Ellen G. White is my spiritual friend. Listen to her counsel:

> *Before the final visitation of God's judgments upon the earth, there will be, among the people of the Lord, such a revival of primitive godliness as has not been witnessed since apostolic times. The Spirit and power of God will be poured out upon His children. At that time many will separate themselves from those churches in which the love of the world has supplanted love for God and His Word. Many, both of ministers and people, will gladly accept those great truths which God has caused to be proclaimed at this time, to prepare a people for the Lord's second coming.[6]*

> *The principles of true spiritual life are not understood by those who know the truth, but fail to practice it. The Lord calls for reforms, marked, distinct reforms. Those in whose hearts Christ dwells will reveal His presence in their dealing with their fellow men. But the principles of some have been so long perverted that they have lost their discernment, and the arrow seldom reaches its mark. How can this be cured? Only by heeding Christ's prayer: "Sanctify them through thy truth, thy word is truth..." (Jn. 17:17-19)[7]*

After sixteen years as a Seventh-day Adventist minister and Seminary professor, I am more convinced than ever that the Seventh-day Adventist Church was raised up by the Lord to spearhead a return to Biblical Christianity! It will be successful in that task because it is determined to stay true to the Word of God. There's no other way. Every popular

---

[6] Ellen G. White, *The Great Controversy*, p.464.

[7] Ellen G . White, *Manuscript #16*, (Feb. 25, 1901).

teaching today, as always, must be tested by the Bible. Opposition to Bible truth can be expected. The more evidence there is, relative to Bible truth, the more opposition can be expected. Why? Because by nature no one, **no one**, wants to accept the personal implications of God's truth.

This Church needs the help of every born-again and Bible believing Christian. It needs your help. Your witness. Your determination to stay true to Scripture, and to the Lord Jesus Christ, no matter what. Has your church fallen? Have you been unhappy because of what you sense is a definite drift away from the Word of God? Follow the Word! Come and join us in the great crusade to recover Biblical Christianity!!

To believers in the Seventh-day Adventist Church Ellen G. White writes:

> *There is no need to doubt, to be fearful that the work will not succeed. God is at the head of the work, and He will set everything in order. If matters need adjusting at the head of the work, God will attend to that, and work to right every wrong. Let us have faith that God is going to carry the noble ship which bears the people of God safely into port.*
>
> *When you think that the work is in danger, pray, "Lord, stand at the wheel. Carry us through the perplexity. Bring us safely into port." Have we not reason to believe that the Lord will bring us through triumphantly?[8]*
>
> *I pray earnestly that the work we do at this time shall impress itself deeply on heart and mind and soul. Perplexities will increase; but let us, as believers in God, encourage one another. Let us not lower the standard, but keep it lifted high, looking unto Him who is the Author and Finisher of our faith.[9]*

Near the desk in my seminary office I keep a wooden bust of Martin Luther. It was carved out of acacia wood by an Igorot woodcarver in the mountains near Baguio in the

---

[8] Ellen G. White, *Selected Messages Book 2*, pp.390-391.

[9] *Ibid*, p.406.

Philippines. I found it one day, while poking around on the basement floor of a native craft shop, hidden in the shadows on the highest shelf.

He is there staring at me day after day, with his implacable look, reminding me of my spiritual heritage. When I look at him I am reminded of his courageous words in the face of the greatest religious power on earth in his day:

> *My conscience is captive to the Word of God. I cannot and I will not recant anything, for to go against conscience is neither right nor safe. God help me. Amen.*[10]

Frederick the Wise, Elector of Saxony was heard to remark: "He is too daring for me."[11]   Such is the spiritual heritage of myself, my wife, and my wife's parents. It is a heritage that flourishes in, and has been honored by the Seventh-day Adventist Church throughout its history. The Seventh-day Adventist Church is determined to stand as firmly upon Scripture as was Luther. Of him Ellen White has written:

> *Zealous, ardent, and devoted, knowing no fear but the fear of God, and acknowledging no foundation for religious faith but the Holy Scriptures, Luther was the man for his time; through him God accomplished a great work for the reformation of the church and the enlightenment of the world.*[12]

The reformation begun by Luther in his day is not over. Our times require an equally daring and strident voice for truth, an equally stubborn adherence to the Word of God. I believe that the Seventh-day Adventist Church is that voice.

You have read my story. I trust it has been a blessing to you, that it has served to inspire you to a more complete surrender to the Lordship of Christ, that you have come to

---

[10] Roland Bainton, *Here I Stand* (New York: Abingdon Press, MCML), p. 185.

[11] *Ibid*, p. 186.

[12] *The Great Controversy*, p. 107.

realize that God has a future and a hope for you that will expand the horizons of your understanding and service. Permit me, finally, to offer you this benediction from the Word of God:

> *And now my little children, stay in happy fellowship with the Lord so that when he comes you will be sure that all is well, and will not have to be ashamed and shrink back from meeting him. Since we know that God is always good and does only right, we may rightly assume that all those who do right are his children.*
> *(1 John 2:28-29, The Living Bible)*

MARANATHA!

TESTIMONIALS

What happens to a book after it is written and published? In particular what happens to a book like this one? Does it have any impact at all? Are hearts and lives touched and even changed by such a witness? Over the years quite a file of testimonials have been received in response to the book. The following are just a few representative examples.

Dear Pastor Holmes,

I am writing you in regard to the book you wrote, Stranger In My Home. *This book was instrumental in bringing me into the Adventist faith. You see, there was a struggle within me for several months, and I wasn't sure why God would be asking me to change religions. I was a Baptist, had been all my life. God led me to some friends who happened to be Adventists. Slowly I started checking things out and became convinced of the truth of the Sabbath first of all.*
No one pushed me. I simply have a questioning mind and I was looking for answers. God really answered some prayers for me in order to show me the way He wanted me to go. You see, I'm pretty stubborn. I would ask for direct answers and God would provide them either through a book or someone speaking to me. It was in June that I finally got around to reading your book. I had heard about it and by accident (?) a copy of it was put in my hands.
I had just gotten back from my first camp meeting and I really felt like I needed to make some sort of decision regarding my religion but I was extremely mixed up and not quite sure of what to do. Late that night I started reading your book and could hardly put it down.

It was amazing because all of the things you were saying in your book were things that had been going on in my mind. I couldn't believe that somebody else had written it out in black and white. Anyway, before I was through reading your book, I was convinced of what I would do. You see, the message in your book was an answer to prayer, it put everything together for me. I stand secure in the decision I made because it was definitely God's leading in a way I had never seen before.

Anyway, I simply wanted to thank you for sharing your struggle in a book so that others could be helped by it.

Dear Pastor Holmes,

I have just finished reading Stranger In My Home, and I feel constrained to write and tell you that it has been a blessing and a refreshment to me.

I too am a Seventh-day Adventist with a Lutheran background. Many years ago God's call was heeded by one of my aunts and its results have benefited many in our family.

My heart thrills at each revelation of truth from the Source of truth. Oh, there's so much to say about the wonders of God's love and His amazing grace! Isn't it marvelous the way God sustained your dear wife during those years of struggle? And how God kept you together! What a testimony to God's ability to bring unity out of division when hearts are totally surrendered to Him. Maranatha!

Dear Pastor Holmes,

Of six new books purchased at Camp Meeting this summer, I chose to read first Stranger In My Home because we heard and knew your story. I have never read a better exposition of our Bible doctrines, or our Spirit of Prophecy, or our philosophies than you have written in this book. But you will be more interested in the blessed help given me by the book.

Last winter it was hard to understand why when my husband was taken the very week the doctor gave him a clean bill of health after a heart attack. I vowed I was going to be <u>very good</u> so that I could surely meet my husband when Jesus comes and stand beside him. Well! As you can guess; I never fell on my face so frequently! As I analyzed "Why?", I suddenly realized I was trying to do it myself on my own works. On my knees, with contrite tears, I sought forgiveness for being so careless.

Then what did I do? Go to another extreme, asking God to heal me so that I could give Bible studies to some of the many on our Pastor's list. Do you see it? I was telling God what I wanted Him to do for me and why He should do it; none of which was my business. How did I learn this time? From the discussion in your book about submission to God. Again, with contrite tears, I pleaded for forgiveness for my lack of holding Him sacred.

Thus, you put my feet on the path of true submission: Thy will be my will and Thy way my way.

Thank you for writing this beautiful book for us. I believe it has put me on the true road of prayer after weeks and weeks of fumbling.

Dear Pastor Holmes,

Both my husband and I just finished reading your book Stranger In My Home and we were thrilled from beginning to end! As you have discovered what a wonderful message we have, it is ever a thrill to hear others discover it too.

I had to laugh at your statement where you mentioned that your wife's friend and the church seemed to keep her well supplied with books faster than you could dispose of them. I have literally inundated a friend of mine with literature and books because she recognized our quality literature and enjoyed it.

Therefore, after reading your book I just had to send it to her for her husband to read. She said she would forward it on to his sister's husband who is a minister.

Thanks again for the delightful story, and much praise and courage to your wife for recognizing truth and following it regardless of the seeming consequences! Her courage will be an inspiration to many other wives, I'm sure.

145

OTHER BOOKS
BY POINTER PUBLICATIONS

NO TURNING BACK
Shirley S. Holmes

After eighteen years Mrs. Holmes, in **NO TURNING BACK** , shares her dramatic story of becoming a Seventh-day Adventist. What was it like for the faithful wife of a Lutheran minister to be confronted by the Adventist message preached by evangelist Joe Crews at a campmeeting in Wisconsin? What were the factors that contributed to the development of the kind of character and personality capable of taking a courageous stand for Bible truth in the face of strong opposition? These, and many other questions, are answered by the author in her own delightful and readable style.

NO TURNING BACK is actually the sequel to **STRANGER IN MY HOME,** and is in response to numerous requests for Mrs. Holmes own story.

To order your copy send a check for $6.95 to

POINTER Publications
10623 Red Bud Trail
Berrien Springs, MI 49103

BOILED RICE AND GLUTEN
C. Raymond Holmes

AUDIO CASSETTES

FAREWELL SERMONS

In high quality audio sound POINTER Publications offers the last five sermons preached by Pastor C. Raymond Holmes to the congregation of Sharon Lutheran Church.

What could Pastor Holmes say to his people prior to leaving for Andrews University and study at the Seventh-day Adventist Theological Seminary? How could he prepare his congregation for the possible outcome of his investigation of Adventist theology?

You can participate in the final dramatic moments of Pastor Holmes' ministry to the congregation he loved!

Set of three tapes $15.95

YOU CAN MAKE IT!

After more than ten years as a pastor and professor in the Seventh-day Adventist Church, Dr. Holmes preaches this challenging series of camp meeting messages from the book of Joshua. Based on the ancient experience of Israel in crossing the Jordan River and occupying the promised land, the series explores the message and mission of the Seventh-day Adventist Church as it faces the challenges of the immediate future.

In the experience of conquering the land of Israel can be found the principles that will guide the last day Church to complete victory and fulfillment. Sermon titles are: *"Facing Your Challenge," "Strategy For The Struggle," "Perspective Provides Power," "Turbulence Trains Troops," "Troops That Triumph," "Saved By A Thread," "How To Fail To Fall,"* and *"You Can Win and Still Lose."* Individual tapes are $5.00 each.

Set of eight tapes $30.00

Send your order to POINTER Publications
10623 Red Bud Trail
Berrien Springs, Mich. 49103

Recorded on high quality cassette tapes

POSTAGE PAID ORDER FORM

Please send me the following:

#1 _____ copies of *Stranger In My Home*, $6.95 each.

#2 _____ copies of *No Turning Back*, $6.95 each.

#3 _____ copies of *Baptized But Buried Alive*, $5.95 each.

#4 _____ copies of *Boiled Rice and Gluten*, $4.95 each.

AUDIO CASSETTES

_____ set(s) of *Farewell Sermons* (3 tapes), $15.95

_____ set(s) of *You Can Make It* (8 tapes), $30.00. Dr. Holmes challenging camp meeting series on the book of Joshua. Individual tapes $5.00 each.

PACKAGE OFFERS

_____ Books #1 and #2, $10.95 (retail $13.90)

_____ Books #3 and #4, $8.95 (retail $10.90)

_____ All four books, $20.95 (retail $24.80)

_____ Book #1 and *Farewell Sermons*, $17.95 (ret. $22.90)

_____ Books #1, #2, and *Sermons*, $23.95 (ret. $29.85)

_____ All four books and *Sermons*, $30.95 (ret. $39.80)

_____ All four books and both Audio Cassettes, *Farewell Sermons* and *You Can Make It*, $45.00 (ret. $74.80)

Name _____ Address _____

City _____ State _____ Zip _____

Mail your order to: POINTER Publications
10623 Red Bud Trail
Berrien Springs, Mich. 49103

Write for discount on ten copies or more of each book